Digital Creature Rigging

Wings, Tails & Tentacles for Animation & VFX

T0133543

Digital Creature Rigging

Wings, Tails & Tentacles for Animation & VFX

Stewart Jones

CRC Press
Taylor & Francis Group
Boca Raton London New York

CRC Press is an imprint of the
Taylor & Francis Group, an **informa** business

A CHAPMAN & HALL BOOK

CRC Press
Taylor & Francis Group
6000 Broken Sound Parkway NW, Suite 300
Boca Raton, FL 33487-2742

Printed on acid-free paper

International Standard Book Number-13: 978-1-138-56069-7 (Paperback)
978-1-138-56070-3 (Hardback)

Library of Congress Cataloging-in-Publication Data

Names: Jones, Stewart, 1984- author.
Title: Digital creature rigging : wings, tails & tentacles for animation & VFX / Stewart Jones.
Description: Boca Raton : Taylor & Francis, a CRC title, part of the Taylor & Francis imprint, a member of the Taylor & Francis Group, the academic division of T&F Informa, plc, 2019.
Identifiers: LCCN 2019004834| ISBN 9781138560697 (paperback : alk. paper) | ISBN 9781138560703 (hardback : alk. paper)
Subjects: LCSH: Rigging (Computer animation) | Computer drawing—Special effects. | Figure drawing. | Characters and characteristics--Computer simulation. | Three-dimensional imaging. | 3ds max (Computer file)
Classification: LCC TR897.7 .J6645 2019 | DDC 006.6/96--dc23
LC record available at https://lccn.loc.gov/2019004834

**Visit the Taylor & Francis Web site at
http://www.taylorandfrancis.com**

**and the CRC Press Web site at
http://www.crcpress.com**

Contents

Preface

Welcome back!

No, you didn't miss anything, you're not starting at the wrong section, you haven't jumped to the wrong chapter – this is the beginning, but it's not THE beginning. You see, over 10 years ago, the idea for *Digital Creature Rigging* was born. At that time, I was rigging anything and everything that was thrown at me. Rigs for film, TV, commercials, video games, medical videos, mechanical demos, experimental rigs; it didn't matter, I was rigging it. Cars, animals, digital doubles, hero characters, trains, planes, crazy make-believe characters; you name it, I probably created some kind of setup for it. I'd jump and switch between Autodesk Maya and Autodesk 3ds Max – scripting in Python or MEL in Maya, and using MAXScript in 3ds Max. I was part of amazing teams doing great things in 3D, and although using both Maya and Max was challenging at times, it was a lot of fun and gave me a unique overview on how the foundations and methods of rigging in three dimensions could be used in both of these great software applications.

I learnt a lot from this experience, and by using these different 3D content creation tools, I was able to solidify my workflows and best practices. How one application had a certain pipeline or order for doing things, the other would be different, but the techniques could be the same for both – it just took some creative thinking. This sparked my idea for the "Creature Toolbox," an auto-rigger: a set of scripts, tools and plugins that could instantly create rigs for many kinds of characters and creatures. I started small at first, building my core scripts in Maya and then replicating them in Max. Time passed and I had an auto-rigger that could build biped rigs (humans) in both Maya and Max, and they behaved exactly the same or as close to the same as was possible. If you learnt how to animate my rigs in Maya, then you would be comfortable animating the same rig in 3ds Max, and vice versa. I then expanded things further – quadrupeds (four-legged animals), aquatics (fish and marine life), avian (birds and flying mammals) and then branching out into modular auto-rigs. This gave incredible and crazy opportunities, and rigs could be created quickly and time spent in more complex areas or looking into shot-specific setups where incredibly precise or special controls were needed for just a few scenes in the production. With the modular rigging system, it opened a lot of possibilities up – you could put a wing on a fish, a fin on a human, and any other combination of prescripted rigs that were part of the Creature Toolbox. It took years to develop into a solid and stable toolkit able to work for an endless amount of situations.

The reason it was called the Creature Toolbox was because creatures were the thing I enjoyed rigging and creating the most. Fantastical beasts, mythical monsters and spectacular specimens – these kinds of creatures still fascinate me. Now, that's not to say that rigging other things doesn't interest me; they do and it does, but for some reason I keep coming back to the creatures. So, I looked for references, help and tutorials on creature rigging. I found some great ones, both online and in books. Some for 3ds Max, but many more for Maya.

Nearly all focused on a single output – either games or film. Why? I thought. Sure, there are differences, but there are more similarities than actual discrepancies.

During my time setting up my Creature Toolbox, I had developed a system that used three stages to set up a rig which would have the same controls, no matter which output the rig was going to be used for. These three stages are:

1. Base rig
2. Animation rig
3. Deformation rig

This got me pondering other aspects of 3D and these three stages that seemed to have some big relevance on the things I was creating. Interestingly, these three stages were completely transferable to other areas of the pipeline, all departments and even down to specific tasks. For instance – a modeler will block out a model (1). They will refine and detail it (2). Finally, they will polish and clean (3). Three stages. An animator will block the animation (1). They will then spline it (2). And then they will polish (3). Again, three stages. I now push these three stages for all disciplines, and I like to use the term "3-Stage Asset Build (3SAB)."

I was still longing to do something with creatures, something for myself and something I could really share with others. So, armed with my experience, this 3SAB technique and a love for all things creature-related, I put together a book proposal and sent it out. As I waited to hear back, Digital-Tutors, now Pluralsight (www.pluralsight.com), offered great online video training for 3ds Max, Maya and many other software applications. I had already created Maya training courses, both at work and for the now retired TD-College, amongst others, so I thought I'd create something for Digital-Tutors too. I decided to work in 3ds Max and develop an advanced rigging course for a cartoon shark that covered manual and automated animation controls. When I finished, I was given the opportunity to author another video class, and I jumped at the opportunity. This was another

3ds Max course, this time on advanced rigging for cars. They were both fun to create, and they're still available on the Pluralsight website if you would like to check them out. Oh, and the tips, tricks and techniques used in those videos are still applicable today, even in the latest versions of Autodesk 3ds Max.

Eventually, I heard back about my book proposal. I was going to be the author of a book which covered rigging 3D creatures. Contracts were agreed and signed; then the work began.

My first stop was recruitment! I asked a good friend of mine, Chris Rocks, if he would lend me his crazy skills to model and texture a creature for this book. He jumped on board, and after some amazing wizardry, he created the fantastic Belraus creature that became the main feature. Weeks passed, and I worked on the rig. Months passed, and I worked on the words and images. Eventually, a fully rigged creature and a completed manuscript left my hands and headed out into the world.

That book is called *Digital Creature Rigging: The Art and Science of CG Creature Setup in 3ds Max* (Jones, 2012), as shown in Figure 0.1.

Figure 0.1

Digital Creature Rigging: The Art and Science of CG Creature Setup in 3ds Max (2012).

It forms the first book in this series, and that is where our adventure first began. So, welcome back to the world of rigging three-dimensional creatures.

Although this book that you're reading right now can be used as a guide on its own, I would suggest that if you haven't checked out the first *Digital Creature Rigging* book, you really should. The foundations, techniques and concepts are all covered in there, and we will be building on those foundations and core methodologies as we move through this book.

Additionally, if you're working through the *Digital Creature Rigging* collection, I should point out that I have a number of other publications out in the world. One of them in particular covers mechanical and technical rigging in 3ds Max – think chains, cogs, belts, pistons, wires and a few other setups for complex machinery. This book is called *Mechanical Creations in 3D: A Practical Look into Complex and Technical Setups for Animation & VFX* (Jones, 2018) and is worth getting hold of for tips, tricks and guides relating to hard-surface rigging. It uses similar techniques to both of the *Digital Creature Rigging* books and serves as a guide as to how the same principles we cover throughout this text can be used on pretty much anything and everything when it comes to rigging.

So, once again – welcome back to *Digital Creature Rigging*. I'm very happy that you're here with me and are jumping back into our continuing journey in three-dimensional awesomeness! As before, I've recruited the incredibly talented Mr. Chris Rocks, and his creatures feature as our main subjects for our journey into *Digital Creature Rigging: Wing, Tails and Tentacles for Animation & VFX*.

Without any further delay, let's get to it!

References

Jones, S. 2012. *Digital Creature Rigging: The Art and Science of CG Creature Setup in 3ds Max*. Boca Raton, FL: CRC Press.

Jones, S. 2018. *Mechanical Creations in 3D: A Practical Look into Complex and Technical Setups for Animation and VFX*. Boca Raton, FL: CRC Press.

Acknowledgments

I am extremely grateful to a number of people who have supported me throughout the years and to a select few who have really helped to make this publication a reality:

- Marie, you are everything to me. I owe you my life, literally. Thank you for all of the moments that we share, all of the laughs that we have, and all of your never-ending support through the best and worst of times. I love you and I love spending my life with you.
- My parents, Carol and Keith. Without your love, help and support, I would be lost. Thank you for everything, past, present and future. Knowing that you are always there for me, no matter which part of the world I'm in, has given me the opportunities and the courage to succeed.
- Chris Rocks… You did it again! Your work is incredible, and I am forever in your debt for the time, effort and dedication that you put into these projects. I'm honored to call you my friend, and huge congratulations to both you and Dawn. Cheers!
- Tina O'Hailey, thank you once again for helping me get the "yes" for another book project. I owe you a coffee if we ever get to meet.
- The original *Digital Creature Rigging* and this book wouldn't have been created without the help of Dave Bevans. Thank you for always being approachable and for pointing me in the right direction. I hope to be able to work with you again.
- Many thanks, Sean Connelly and Jessica Vega, my team of top editors! You guys made this possible and I appreciate everything you've done for me.

There are so many other people I have to thank for many things and my apologies for not being able to include everyone here, but I hope you all know how grateful I am to each and every one of you. Finally, my thanks to you for reading. I appreciate you being here and taking this journey into three-dimensional rigging with me.

Author

Stewart Jones is a writer, screenwriter, producer and director, with experience in feature film, TV, TVC, video games and VR/AR. As an accomplished creative professional, his background includes animation, live action and visual effects (VFX) productions for worldwide clients. He is a full member of the Writers' Guild of Great Britain (WGGB), a published author and journal-published MBA graduate.

Currently, Stewart works as an independent freelancer providing writing, screenwriting, producing and directing services for international clients and productions. Additionally, Stewart holds training workshops throughout the year and can often be found speaking or teaching online and at various international conferences, colleges and events. His previous roles include everything from animator to technical director (TD), and computer graphics (CG) supervisor or head of 3D to production manager.

For more information on Stewart, please check out the following links:

Personal Website: www.creatureattic.com
Twitter: twitter.com/creatureattic
LinkedIn: linkedin.com/in/stewart-jones/
Amazon Author: amazon.com/Stewart-Jones/e/B0091IL2U4
IMDb: imdb.me/stewartjones
WGGB: writersguild.org.uk/profile/?profile=2992

Contributor

As I mentioned in the Acknowledgments section already, I really couldn't have created such an incredible steampunk train without the hard work and dedication of my good friend, Chris Rocks. I've worked with Chris for a number of years on many different projects, and I'm proud to say that he is my go-to 3D artist for anything and everything.

I've been lucky enough to have Chris's assistance in the following three publications, which includes this one:

Jones, S. 2012. *Digital Creature Rigging: The Art and Science of CG Creature Setup in 3ds Max.* Boca Raton, FL, CRC Press.

Jones, S. 2018. *Mechanical Creations in 3D: A Practical Look into Complex and Technical Setups for Animation and VFX.* Boca Raton, FL, CRC Press.

Jones, S. 2019. *Digital Creature Rigging: Wings, Tails & Tentacles for Animation & VFX.* Boca Raton, FL, CRC Press.

Chris is available for freelance work, and I highly recommend him for any 3D production. Really, this guy is just the best! But, don't take my word for it – here is a short profile so you get a better understanding about him:

Chris has more than 20 years digital experience in video games, TVC, marketing, advertising, education, medical, design and VR/AR. In that time he has worked on multiple award-winning productions, including being an integral part of two Bafta-winning projects. As a digital creative, his varied background has included working with UK and globally renowned brands in a multitude of roles.

Currently, Chris is a contract 3D visualizer working for an international technology company specializing in product development. His previous roles have included everything from 3D artist to creative director (CD), and computer graphics (CG) supervisor or art production manager.

For more information on Chris, please check out the following links:

Personal Website: www.tartanpimpernel.com
LinkedIn: linkedin.com/in/tartanpimpernel/

1

Introduction

Rigging in 3ds Max, Maya, Houdini, Blender or any other 3D software is all the same – a series of hierarchies with specific controllers to manipulate its specific elements.

Stewart Jones

The world of computer graphics (CG), 3D, animation and visual effects (VFX) is changing as rapidly as ever. Advances in technology, new software and state-of-the-art hardware allow for continuously improving final images, either static or moving, in print, onscreen and even in various realities like virtual and augmented reality. Finished projects and productions can look more incredible, feel more believable, and distort our view on what's real and what is fake. It's an exciting time to be part of this field, but what is surprising is that the core fundamentals, the true basics of CG, haven't changed one bit. For me, this is both very disappointing and somewhat concerning.

When *Digital Creature Rigging: The Art and Science of CG Creature Setup in 3D* was first published, way back in 2012, the foundations of rigging in three dimensions hadn't really changed for a long time. Sure, there were some new tools and new techniques added to the software, things like dual-quaternion skinning,

1

which was a relatively new development, and Python was quickly taking over as the main scripting language used in productions, amongst others. But, at the very root of everything, rigging in 3D was still just the same.

Need a biped character? Rig it! Inverse kinematics (IK), forward kinematics (FK), joints/bones, and reverse foot setups – it was and still is the same. Animation studios, VFX studios, they're all using similar setups for similar characters. Yet these frameworks are either custom-scripted auto-riggers or built manually, but they all behave similarly. Of course, some productions are using out-of-the-box auto-riggers like Biped or CAT, which are built into Autodesk 3ds Max, but they can feel more limited than custom creations. This often forces character/creature technical directors (TDs) and riggers to create their own systems. Heck, I even have my own scripted system for these things, as I mentioned earlier!

What I'm trying to say is that once you've learnt the basics, it's really all the same. At least, it is until you're asked to work on an octopus that can walk on land. Or a bird that has to open and close its wings onscreen with realistic feathers. Okay, now we are talking about some exciting challenges that are going to require some very unique setups.

Wings, tails and tentacles; some of the most problematic areas of creature setup that provide challenges to even those most experienced with rigging and setups in 3D. Those things, along with shoulders, of course! These problems, otherwise known as challenges, need to be solved in such a way that our control mechanisms are simple, logical and easy to use for an animation team. This is easier said than done, as some of these kinds of rigs are tricky and complicated to implement. But, this book is here to help out, so no worries.

As you work your way through this book, you'll be digging into techniques that aren't often covered in rigging tutorials. We are building on the foundations set out in the first *Digital Rigging* book (Jones, 2012), which means that we can rush through the basics of setting up creatures and really dive in and explore the more advanced and complex topics.

Our first challenge is a watery squid creature! Its tentacles and jellylike body are going to cause us squishy, squashy, stretchy, moldable troubles. Then we move onto a mythical dragon, which makes us focus on wing setups that need to move and deform realistically, giving us another challenging rigging task.

Like the first book, we are once again sticking with Autodesk 3ds Max to create the rigs for these creatures. As such, we cover techniques specific to this software. And, just as before, the concepts presented really are universal and can be applied to any 3D application. Tools and names will be different, of course, but everything else should be the same. I don't say this without research, either, as I am a user of both Autodesk 3ds Max and Autodesk Maya and my rigs turn out pretty much identical no matter which program I end up working in.

At the time of writing this, the latest version of 3ds Max is Autodesk 3ds Max 2019. As such, this is the version that I'll personally be using throughout this book. I strongly believe that the techniques used throughout this text are transferrable to older versions of the software, so there is no need to worry if you don't have access to the same version that I'm using. Additionally, if you're using a newer version, I'm pretty confident that all of the techniques and methods used for the rigging of the creatures in this book will transfer over just fine.

Oh, and one last thing. For the purposes of these rigs, I don't use any additional scripts or fancy plugins. These creatures are built using a standard 3ds Max setup – the exact one that you get when you grab hold of 3ds Max for the first time.

1.1 Chapter Overview

This book is separated into 10 chapters, with each chapter covering theoretical concepts and practical guides which aim to solidify the theory. By the end of these chapters, we will have completed a squid and dragon rig using a number of techniques, tools and skills.

- Chapter 1: "Introduction"
  - You're looking at Chapter 1 right now! This is the main introduction to this book, where we summarize what we are going to be covering as well as discussing some of the core fundamentals and methodologies that are used throughout this text.
- Chapter 2: "The Creatures"
  - Before jumping into the complexities of the rigging process, we take time in Chapter 2 to discuss, analyze and become acquainted with the two creatures that feature on the front cover and throughout. We dig into the geometry of each creature and make notes on the challenges, problems and types of controls that we are going to need to create in order to complete both of the needed rigs.
- Chapter 3: "Rigging Preparations"
  - We spend some time in this chapter preparing both of the creature models for rigging. This includes making sure that the geometry and scenes are clean while adding in some preliminary rigging work for the upcoming chapters and rigging stages.
- Chapter 4: "Pheridan: Base Rig"
  - In Chapter 4, we start rigging the first of our creatures, Pheridan. This squid creature needs to have its bones and base hierarchy completed before moving into basic skinning of the geometry so that we can move ahead into the animation rigging phase.
- Chapter 5: "Pheridan: Animation Rig"
  - The challenging animation rig for the Pheridan creature has us looking into two main sections, the torso/spine area and the limbs. For each of the limbs, we look into various approaches that can be used to rig this creature depending on the needs of your productions.
- Chapter 6: "Pheridan: Deformation Rig"
  - Pheridan's deformation rig takes us through a basic face setup, then into various options to help with problematic surface deformations.

From there, this chapter moves into applying tools to create automated limb movements in order to simulate swimming and overlapping action.

- Chapter 7: "Xilteor: Base Rig"
  - Following similar steps to Pheridan's base rig, this chapter takes us through the steps we need to complete to make sure that Xilteor is ready for the animation rig. We create the base hierarchy and then look into bone and controller placement. We finish by taking care of skinning deformations so that everything is ready for the next chapter.
- Chapter 8: "Xilteor: Animation Rig"
  - Xilteor's animation rig covers overlapping inverse kinematics before we create a custom geometry spline IK system to control the main mass of the creature. Our last task here is to take care of the wings, and we do this with a simple forward kinematics system attached to a specific hierarchical structure which we can use in the next chapter.
- Chapter 9: "Xilteor: Deformation Rig"
  - It is during this chapter that we revisit the deformations of Xilteor's geometry and add some extra controls for a simple face rig. The bulk of our time is spent looking into three methods to automate wing flapping, wing folding and overlapping action. It is during the implementation of these methods that we use a number of different tools and various techniques to complete the dragon creature rig.
- Chapter 10: "Conclusion"
  - The final chapter of this book allows me to congratulate you on your journey, reiterate information on the various files that we use throughout this book and even take a look at the book's cover image. We round things out by discussing the *Digital Creature Rigging* book series, the creatures within them and even another book which may be helpful for you if you're interested in working on mechanical setups.

1.2 Digital Creature Rigging

At its core, and as the first book in this series is subtitled – digital creature rigging is the art and science of CG rigging setups in 3D. It's the concepts, methods, techniques, skills and stages that go into the creation of production-ready creature rigs for film, TV and video games. The strategies outlined allow us to create creature rigs of all types and make them easily ready for automatic use in many different types of media (transmedia) – think one rig to do it all. It is the practical, hands-on approaches that help with the development and creation of believable creature rigs.

Digital Creature Rigging: The Art and Science of CG Creature Setup in 3ds Max (Jones, 2012) covers all of the tools, tricks and foundations needed to succeed in creating advanced creature rigs. This book, *Digital Creature Rigging: Wings, Tails and Tentacles*, enhances those fundamentals, adapts them, updates them where needed, relies upon them and uses them in the creation of rigging areas which are often not covered in other methodologies.

1.3 Artistic and Scientific

Split into hemispheres, each side of the human brain is responsible for different things. The left side of the brain is where we calculate logic, mathematics, language, reading, writing and analysis (science). The right side controls personality, creativity, intuition, music, art and spatial abilities (art). When it comes to rigging creatures, we need to rely on both hemispheres.

We are required to mix both art and science to create believable rigs that are often complex, but need to be intuitive and easy to use. Jumping between the left and right hemisphere is not always easy, but it starts to become second nature over time. Much of what we do needs to be artistically and visually appealing while being technically competent and robust. Rigging is not unlike most other areas of 3D, but the split between the left and right sides of the brain is pretty even, which is very different from other related disciplines.

1.4 Twelve Rigging Principles

We covered the rigging principles in the first *Digital Creature Rigging* book, where I attempted to create a set of 12 rigging principles that could be used for creating any kind of rigs in 3D. An in-depth look at these principles can be found in that text, and we'll once again stick to these principles:

1. KISS! – Keep It Simple, Stupid!
2. Planning
3. Research, Development, Resources
4. Anatomy
5. Biomechanics
6. Flesh-Surface Deformations
7. Animation
8. Modeling
9. Pipeline
10. Dynamics
11. Scripting
12. Mathematics

1.5 Naming Conventions

As always, naming conventions are as important as ever. It took a good amount of time to come up with a naming convention that could be used in pretty much any application, in any folder/operating system and any situation. However, the time that was invested to make sure that these are as robust as possible definitely paid off. Due to this effort, I've used these naming conventions for well over five years now, and they haven't let me down yet. In fact, they are exactly the same as they were in the first *Digital Creature Rigging* book, with a few additions as they have been required as I've been working on newer projects.

Formatting for this naming convention is as follows:

CATEGORY_itemNameNumber_SIDE_TYPE

As you can see, the name of anything and everything created in the scene will consist of five specific elements:

1. *Category*: The category of the object. Required for each object.
2. *Item Name*: The actual name of the object. This is a requirement.
3. *Number*: If item numbering is needed, this is where it goes. We use a three-digit (000) style for this.
4. *Side*: Left or right? Upper or lower? This is where we specify, but this is optional.
5. *Type*: What type of object is it? This is also required information.

You can obviously use your own naming convention as you work through this text, but I really recommend taking a look over this system and considering which works best for you. To explain things a little better, Table 1.1 breaks down these five elements in greater detail.

If the amazing awesomeness of these naming conventions wasn't enough to behold, I have another super-incredible thing to share with you. I'd like to introduce you to the idea, the concept, the practical implementation and the really cool thing to have in your office or at home... Please welcome the Convention Cube (Figure 1.1).

The Convention Cube is the complete naming convention mapped to the sides of a box. Now, this is available as a 3D model, but this was never the intention of its creation. In fact, while I worked at Relentless Software, a videogames company in the United Kingdom, we printed the net of this cube and built them. Multiple Convention Cubes were placed around the office so that literally everyone had easy access to see the naming conventions we used for all projects. I really recommend this approach. It's helpful for new team members to come to grips with the way things are named, and it helps to keep experienced crew members in check. Now, these Convention Cubes don't cover everything, and as the text on these cubes states – if in doubt, ask!

The net and the 3D asset for the Convention Cube are included with the resources of this book; all you have to do is head on over to the companion website (www.DigitalRigging.com) and navigate your way to find the assets for this book. This cube was created some time ago, so there may be a few changes to the details, but it is generally a solid reference, and you can always update things if you would like to (or even create your own). Oh, and as a side note

Table 1.1 Naming Conventions

CATEGORY_itemNameNumber_SIDE_TYPE	
CATEGORY (Required)	
CAM	Camera
CH	Character
ENV	Environment
FX	Effect/Particle/Emitter
LI	Light
OBJ	Object or Prop
GUI	Graphical User Interface
GLOBAL	Shared by Multiple Categories

itemName (Required) [Multiple]
Item names can be anything and everything that you want them to be. If you have more than one item name, use the minus (−) symbol to split, but use this sparingly so that the item name length is reasonable.

itemNumber (Optional) [Single]
Always use three (3) digits for item numbering. Example, *001*.

SIDE (Optional) [Single]
If more clarity is needed, sides can be combined.

L	Left
C	Right
R	Center
LWR	Lower
UPR	Upper

TYPE (Required) [Multiple]	
ANIM	Animation
AS	Animation Set
AT	Animation Tree
BS	Blendshape/Morph Target
BRANCH	Second-Level Hierarchical Parent
CAM	Camera
CTRL	Controller
DATA	Data Node
GEO	Geometry
IK	Inverse Kinematic Chain
JNT	Joint/Bone
LI	Light
LINE	Spline/Curve/Line
LOC	Locator/Dummy/Point Helper
MAT_(D/N/S)	Material (Diffuse/Normal/Specular)
PA	Physics Asset
PFX	Particle System
RIG	Rigging Specific
ROOT	Hierarchical Parent (No other type suffix required)
TEMP	Temporary Item
UTIL	Utility Node

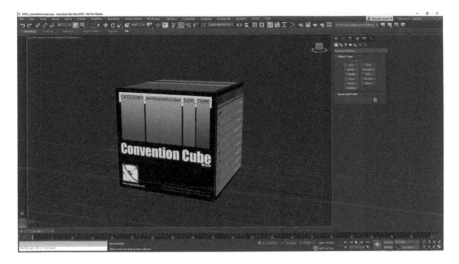

Figure 1.1

The Convention Cube is a 3D model which can be printed and assembled in paper for your desk as a visual reminder of the naming conventions.

– Relentless Software closed its doors permanently in 2016, years after I left the company. It was a great place to be, and the talented team there was amazing. I miss those peeps!

1.6 Colors

Along with a strict naming convention comes a specific color code for all elements in the rig, but this is a little simpler. For elements in the center, they are colored yellow. Taking the lead from maritime and aircraft vehicles, we color elements on the **left** in red, and elements on the right in green. Any additional elements which are core sections of the setup are blue, and any **extras** which don't form any of the core sections can be any color imaginable—I usually go with a white or purple! (See Table 1.2.)

Table 1.2 Colors

COLORS	
CENTER	Objects in the center
LEFT	Objects on the left
RIGHT	Objects on the right
ADDITIONAL	Extra objects that are part of the core element
EXTRA	Extra objects that are *not* part of the core element

1. Introduction

1.7 Display Layers

We have so many options in 3ds Max when it comes to manipulating the display of objects in our scenes. I combine a number of these to lock away or hide certain objects away from animator's hands – or from anyone who might be working with my rigs and may inadvertently break them by accessing objects which shouldn't be there. One of my favorite ways of controlling the display of objects is to use the built-in *Display Layers*. There is a default layer already created for us, but I like to add additional layers in there which will eventually contain specific objects so that I know where everything is. It's really just another great scene-management technique.

For all of my rigs, I include the following display layers:

- 0 (Default)
  - The default layer which cannot be removed.
- ANIM
  - Animation layer.
- BS
  - Blendshapes/morph targets.
- CAM
  - Cameras.
- CTRL
  - Rig controls.
- DATA
  - Data and stored data layer.
- DEFORM
  - Deformation objects.
- FX
  - Effects and particles.
- GEO
  - Geometry.
- LI
  - Lights and illumination objects.
- MSCLE
  - Objects or plugins used for muscle simulation.
- RIG
  - Rigging-specific objects (IK, splines, etc.).
- SKEL
  - Joints/Bones.
- WIP
  - An area for work-in-progress setups/objects.

1.8 Layered Setups

Layered setups are a basic methodology which I always use when rigging. It gets no more complicated than thinking of building blocks being stacked upon each other. Each layer is needed as a foundation for the next, and the next is more visible (to the audience) than the last.

Imagine four building blocks. The first is the most difficult to change, as the others are resting upon it; the last building block is the easiest to change, as it is has the other building blocks which are supporting it. The thing is, from the audience's perspective, the last building block is the most important, as it is the one that they see. This makes the first building bock the least important – from the view of the audience – but for us, they are all important. Hang on, this should make things clearer and more apparent for rigging; see Figure 1.2.

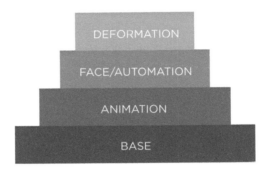

Figure 1.2

Layered setups for rigging. Each layer builds upon the last.

1.9 3-Stage Asset Build

Sometimes things can get overwhelming. When there are a million things to do, knowing which thing to start first can be difficult. Rigging is one of those things that has so many different tasks that it can seem like a daunting task to build a great rig. I like to break down these tasks, and I mean any and all tasks, into three specific stages.

These stages can be used as mini-goals, which we can aim for as we work through the larger task – no matter what that task is. It also acts as a point to schedule against as well as where we can track progress. Additionally, and equally important, is the fact that these stages can be bridging points between disciplines – it's a point where we can hand over the current progress to another department, where they can start working and we can continue to the next milestone without fear of slowing down the big machine that is the project.

Hopefully, that makes a lot of sense from both a personal development point of view, as well as from a production and pipeline aspect. So, how do we break down this 3-stage asset build, or 3SAB? Well, it's easy:

1. *Blocking*: This is where we start from. We create anything and everything that is needed for the final asset without all of the fancy bells and whistles. We're

aiming for everything to be technically solid and ready for the production pipeline.

2. *Refinement*: With our asset already moving through the production pipeline, we can work on the refinements to the technically solid "Blocking" phase. This should mean that when we complete this stage, our asset is close to being completed and we only need to add the extras to take it from good to great.

3. *Polish*: At this point, we're making any final changes and edits while polishing and perfecting details. Once this phase is complete, we should be able to let go of the asset and move on to the next.

1.10 Film/TV Rigs vs Video Game Rigging

Creating rigs for video games or real-time rendering only? Then it is impossible to include all of the deformers and tricks that film rigs are able to use. In fact, you have to make things look incredible with a very limited toolset and many restrictions. If you're rigging your creatures for film and TV or any prerendered outputs, it makes no sense to limit the tools on offer like a video game rig has to. Anything and everything can be used to make the rigs look fantastic.

But, what about creating a film rig that may need a video game rig as well? Or perhaps you're creating film rigs that need some kind of real-time elements, like for pre-viz, for instance, or augmented reality (AR) or virtual reality (VR). What about a video game that needs some prerendered work? If this is the case, why not create rigs that can do everything?

Think about it. If you animate a walk cycle in a video game, you can use that exact walk cycle for a prerendered video. Animate a shot for a film, and you can use that exact animation in a real-time engine with little to no trouble at all. As a creature TD, it makes no sense to spend time and effort creating separate rigs. From a production point of view, reusing assets that have already been created makes scheduling easier and more financially sensible. There are options for transferring animation via files and scripts, but we then need to spend additional time researching and developing toolkits that can do this successfully.

I'm an avid supporter of the "one-rig-fits-all" mentality – that is, of course, if it's needed. So, throughout this book and the rigs that we build, I will endeavor to make sure that they can be used for both real-time game engines and prerendered video. This will usually be in the form of baking down movements from animation onto the base rig only, removing the need for the animation rig and its components. It is then just a case of removing computationally heavy deformers that may not be supported in the real-time renderer. These limitations change depending on your engine choice and with newer updates, so it's impossible for me to catch every situation, but I'll do my best to make it usable in things like Unity and Unreal – two very popular engines at the time of writing this.

1.10.1 Shot-Specific Rigging

Referencing directly to additional rigging setups needed for specific situations, shot-specific rigging really comes down to the creation of setups that solve problems or explicit needs for one-off shots. These kind of setups are usually added to a kind of "one-size-fits-all" rig, which is used for the majority of the production. In fact, shot-specific rigging doesn't just have to be for "shots." It can also be used in video games where the standard controls or setup is just not able to handle certain needs. Now, this is by no means a negative reflection on the standard rig; far from it. In fact, the standard rig needs to be usable at least 90% of the time, but that additional 10% may need a little something extra to allow animators to get the control that they really need or to sell the believability of the rig to the audience.

It's important to note that during this book we will be focusing only on the "one-size-fits-all" rig. We will be creating setups that can function and be used for at least 90%, if not 100%, of a production and will be suitable for film, TV, games and AR/VR mediums. Any extras that may be needed are just too specific to be covered in the text, although basic things like adding additional geometry to the models for smoother results will be discussed.

1.11 Companion Website

Just like with the first *Digital Creature Rigging* book, the companion website (Figure 1.3) contains all of the assets that are created throughout this text. It's

Figure 1.3

The companion website. *www.DigitalRigging.com*

totally worth heading over to the site and checking these things out, but remember, this book is written to allow you to use the tips and techniques to be able to build your own creature setups. So, if you do have a creature you're working on, why not try following through using that instead? The creatures from this book are always there for reference should you need them!

Oh, you may notice that this website contains the assets for another book, *Mechanical Creations in 3D – A Practical Look into Complex and Technical Setups for Animation & VFX* (Jones, 2018). This book is not exactly part of the *Digital Creature Rigging* series, but it does closely relate to them, as it uses the same principles and techniques. The big difference? It's not about rigging creatures, it's about rigging hard-surface objects and machines. In particular, a steampunk train named, Norah… It's worth checking out!

1.12 Summary

Great stuff! We've looked over what's coming up, checked out the principles and theories, recapped naming conventions and colors, and found out where the assets for this book are currently living. If you're new to these things, I hope that you've been able to take some notes and come away from this with some insightful information. If this isn't your first time jumping into the *Digital Creature Rigging* universe, I hope this quick refresher solidified this information and emphasized how important these key concepts are to the rigging and creature setup process.

That's really all there is for the basics in this book. We're now ready to really start jumping in and taking on the challenge of these two creatures – a giant squid and a powerful dragon. Let's do this!

References

Jones, S. 2012. *Digital Creature Rigging: The Art and Science of CG Creature Setup in 3ds Max*. Boca Raton, FL: CRC Press.
Jones, S. 2018. *Mechanical Creations in 3D: A Practical Look into Complex and Technical Setups for Animation and VFX*. Boca Raton, FL: CRC Press.

2

The Creatures

What you do today can improve all your tomorrows.

Ralph Marston

We have the pretty big task of building two creature rigs, both of which are very different from each other. The first, a giant squid that has a body with the consistency of jelly and eight tentacles which can squash, stretch, twist and whip their way around the scene. The second, a huge dragon with a body that is very reptilian, similar to a dinosaur, and huge imposing wings that have to flap and fold believably. Even on their own, these creature rigs are challenging, but with some careful preparation and planning, we can tackle these challenges confidently.

However, before we jump into the rigging of these creatures, we're going to spend some time getting acquainted with them. We will take a detailed look at these creatures, followed by an in-depth look at their geometry and the processes that have gone into the creation of these fantastic models. Finally, we'll spend some time to really think about the specifics of those challenges that we're going to be facing when we rig these creatures. These preliminary checks, changes, edits and discussions save us time and headaches further down the line and later in production.

Both of these creatures have been created to live in the same world as each other even though they are very different in terms of their anatomy. The design of these creatures has also been heavily influenced by the needs of this book. What I mean by that is the book's title and core focus – wings, tails and tentacles.

There could have been a number of directions we took this book, but the decision to choose both an aquatic creature, the squid, and an avian creature, the dragon, was an easy one to make. We not only cover the topics needed for this book, but we keep it in a mythical creature realm, which is both fun and challenging. It also gives us the opportunity to revisit some sections of the first *Digital Creature Rigging* book by allowing us to once again look at spines and limbs, and so on. But, it also allows us to expand on those areas by attaching wings, more complicated tail controls and even tentacle setups that need to be able to behave in a number of very specific ways.

2.1 Overview

As with the first *Digital Creature Rigging* book, we will first start by a quick evaluation of the creatures that we are going to rig. This includes a brief profile for the creatures which acts as a fun introduction to their personalities. Of course, this is not really needed, but this profiling actually gives us some valuable information that we can use to evaluate their movements, behaviors and reactions.

From there we can breakdown their anatomical structures and specific attributes that we may need to watch out for while rigging. This will give us the opportunity to work out the joint placement, controller types and controller placement and highlight possible difficulties and challenges that might face us as we move into rigging.

We're always asking and trying to answer a number of questions as we look into the development of our creature rigs:

- What is the physical resemblance of this creature? What in the real world can we use as the closest reference?
- How is this creature going to be used throughout the production? How are they going to move?
- Do we need to provide additional shot-specific rigs for this creature build? Are there any very specific and special movements that need to look great, but only happen once or twice?
- Who is going to be responsible for animating the creature? How do they like their rigs? What specific controls do they want from their rigs?

2.2 Giant Squid: Pheridan

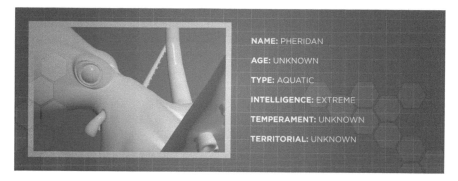

NAME: PHERIDAN

AGE: UNKNOWN

TYPE: AQUATIC

INTELLIGENCE: EXTREME

TEMPERAMENT: UNKNOWN

TERRITORIAL: UNKNOWN

Figure 2.1

Profile: The giant squid – Pheridan.

NAME: Pheridan (Figure 2.1).
AGE: Unknown
TYPE: Aquatic
INTELLIGENCE: Extreme
TEMPERAMENT: Unknown
TERRITORIAL: Unknown
PROFILE: A giant squid found in the very deepest depths of the ocean, only surfacing to attack and destroy anything that affects its surrounding waters. Pheridan (Fur-ay-dan) is a fantasy-style hybrid monster, mostly consisting of a generic squid/octopus build but with no direct reference to a specific breed. Although not much is known about this creature, it is extremely intelligent and capable of propelling itself out of the water to attack its prey.

- *Movement*: Elegant and powerful in the water. Extreme mobility with dynamically stretching and scaling abilities. Out of water, its lack of a skeletal structure makes its movement slower and awkward, often wrapping and twisting itself as it traverses environments. It is significantly less dominant out of the sea.
- *Behavior*: Calm, collected and cunning – Pheridan is extremely intelligent. Attacking only when provoked, every movement is calculated and planned. When comfortable, it moves slowly and precisely.
- *Reaction*: Reacts only after careful consideration of its environment and situation. Generally inquisitive, it will not attack or move unless threatened or directly disturbed.

2.2.1 Pheridan: Anatomy and Attributes

The most obvious real-world creatures to study for their movements, anatomy and attributes are squids, octopi (octopuses if you prefer) and jellyfish. These are at least the most logical and closely related kinds of creatures that we can compare to Pheridan. By using these three as reference, we have something that we can refer to while we rig and it also gives the audience a reference point to relate to when they see this creature animated.

Pheridan has three distinct sections which all need their own special attention even though they all have to work seamlessly together while being able to squish, squash and stretch as we need it to. The first area is the torso, or central section of the creature – I'm sure that there is some kind of correct naming for this, but "torso" works for our purposes (Figure 2.2).

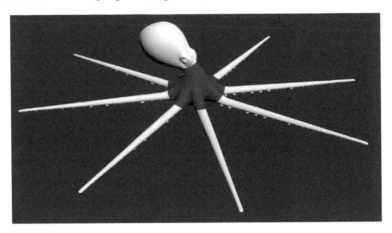

Figure 2.2

The "torso" section of this creature.

This section is where we have the creature's center of gravity (COG) and where all movements should emit from. Under the creature is a kind of beak, which is the mouth for the creature, so we need to spend some time here making sure that works correctly and as we expect it to. On its sides are two exhaustlike structures; we'll need to rig these in some way, but they are not big enough to really cause us too many problems.

Moving upwards, we have the head and eyes for our creature (Figure 2.3). It's in this section that we need to think about making the whole head as flexible as possible while keeping the eyes rigid.

Finally, the tentacles of this creature will need to be able to twist, bend, stretch, squash, flex and do all manner of crazy movements (Figure 2.4). It's going to be a challenge, that's for sure, and even when we have a solution set for each of these "legs," we need to worry about the many suckers attached to the bottom. We have some work to do!

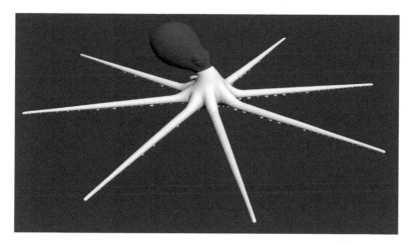

Figure 2.3

The head of Pheridan needs to be very flexible while keeping some rigidity in the eyes.

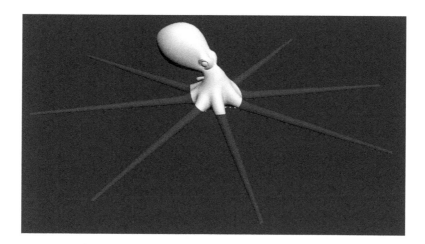

Figure 2.4

The tentacles or "legs" on this creature are going to take us a lot of effort in order to rig properly.

2.2.2 Pheridan: Planning and Preparation

We have a solid idea of the who and what of Pheridan, meaning that we can start documenting our thoughts into a plan of action. I like to start with some images of the creature first, so I quickly grab some screen shots of the model in both shaded and wireframe modes from various angles.

These angles include:

- Isometric (Perspective)
- Front
- Back
- Left
- Right
- Bottom

This should give us 6 images in total, although I render 12 in total – 6 with wireframes and 6 without (Figure 2.5).

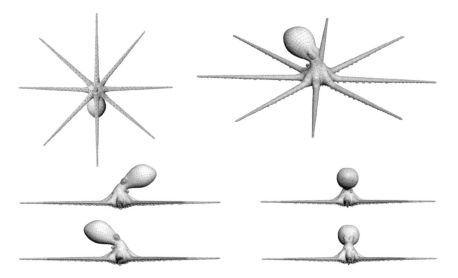

Figure 2.5

Six images of our creature, giving us a blueprint to work from.

At this point, and if it helps you get an idea of the kinds of positions the creature could get into, it might be a good idea to spend some time sketching out thumbnails. However, if you're comfortable with what will be needed for the rig, then we can jump straight into using the 12 creature images we took and create joint placement and controller diagrams. As you can see from Figure 2.6, these are simple rough drawings of where we are going to place everything and what they could possibly look like.

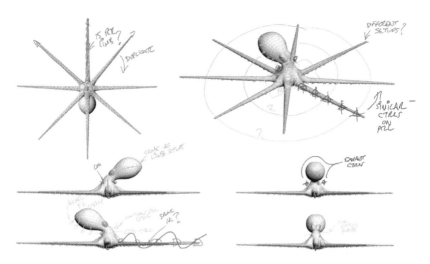

Figure 2.6

The combined joint placement diagram and controller diagram for Pheridan.

2.3 Imposing Dragon: Xilteor

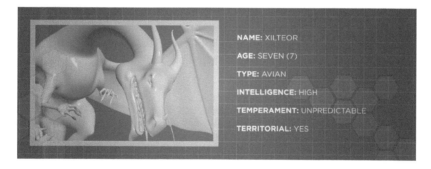

NAME: XILTEOR
AGE: SEVEN (7)
TYPE: AVIAN
INTELLIGENCE: HIGH
TEMPERAMENT: UNPREDICTABLE
TERRITORIAL: YES

Figure 2.7

Profile: The imposing dragon – Xilteor.

> *NAME*: Xilteor (Figure 2.7).
> *AGE*: Seven (7)
> *TYPE*: Avian
> *INTELLIGENCE*: High
> *TEMPERAMENT*: Unpredictable
> *TERRITORIAL*: Yes
> *PROFILE*: This huge beast rules the skies with its impressive wingspan and
> dramatic ability to soar high and far in any kind of weather. On the
> ground, it's more cumbersome and struggles with the unwieldy size of

its wings and the smaller, less powerful front legs. The creature is highly intelligent and acts unpredictably, and once it has marked its den, nothing will stop it from defending it.

- *Movement*: Graceful and highly maneuverable in the skies, Xilteor is able to use its huge and powerful wings to elevate itself to incredible heights. It then uses snakelike motions to twist and turn, giving it very high agility in the air. On the ground, its imposing stance hides its awkward movement as it struggles with the large wingspan and its smaller, less powerful front legs.
- *Behavior*: Xilteor is unpredictable at any time. Calm and sedate in one moment, aggressive and vicious the next. This creature prefers to be alone and it will attack without reason if anyone or anything approaches its chosen den.
- *Reaction*: Always the first to strike, even though it is highly intelligent, it does not consider the consequences of its actions towards other creatures or its environment. If approached by something new or unknown, it will deal deadly attacks before questioning what that thing is.

2.3.1 Xilteor: Anatomy and Attributes

Bats, crocodiles, lizards – these are the first creatures that exist in the real world that come to my mind when compared to Xilteor. What's really great about having a dragon to rig is that there are not only these real-world examples to reference, but there have also been many films and television shows which have very believable dragons in them. So, if they were featured and believable in those shows or films, then we can simply reference their movements, too! I'll not give you a list of possibilities for this. I'm sure that a few movies or episodes come to mind already.

Xilteor has many sections to think about as we break down its anatomical structure and attributes. The torso is where the center of gravity will be placed, down by the hips of the creature. This is where movement will come from and acts as the hub for all of the other sections (Figure 2.8).

Supporting this creature on the ground are its huge rear legs and smaller front legs (Figure 2.9). As both the front and back legs are not the same structures, we will have to approach the rigging of these differently. Oh, and of course there are hands and feet (or claws, if you want to call them that) attached to these supports.

We will spend some time rigging the creature's head and face specifically, but more interesting is the long neck and tail with a huge rear fin (Figure 2.10). This is going to make our rigging considerations interesting as we have to think about how all of these sections, including the torso, fit and work together – especially when we consider that Xilteor's movement in the sky can become snakelike.

Finally, the enormous wings need to be able to flap, fold, gesture and move believably. This is going to be a difficult challenge to rig (Figure 2.11), not so much due to the fact that they are wings, but more because it will be hard to give enough control so that correct movement is possible without creating a crazy amount of controls everywhere.

Figure 2.8

The "torso" section of Xilteor acts as a hub for all of the other sections.

Figure 2.9

Legs and feet allow the creature movement when it is not flying.

Figure 2.10

The head and face will need some special attention when we start to rig it; however, the long neck and tail pose an interesting challenge that we will need to overcome.

Figure 2.11

The wings of Xilteor are going to give us the biggest challenge in this whole rig.

2. The Creatures

2.3.2 Xilteor: Planning and Preparation

As with Pheridan, we need to jump in and grab 12 images using the Print Screen command so that we have some reference of this creature. Remember, these images include views from the left, right, front, back, bottom and isometric (perspective) angles with both shaded and wireframe models (Figure 2.12). You could also take this up to 14 images if you add a top angle in there, it's up to you.

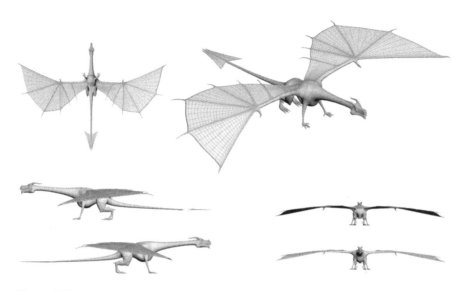

Figure 2.12

These six images will help us do some planning for the upcoming rigging sections.

Once again, you could spend some time sketching out thumbnails for this character to get a better understanding of the deformations that this model will be getting into. I'm once again just leaving this up to my research and reference, as there is a lot of it available out there and I have a pretty good idea of how I'm going to approach this rig. It's probably worth mentioning that I'm not just guessing things here; I've rigged a number of flying creatures before, so I'll be using knowledge from those previous rigs to help me out with things as we go ahead.

The last thing is to create the joint placement and controller diagrams (Figure 2.13).

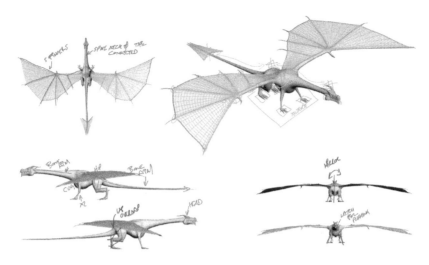

Figure 2.13

The combined joint placement diagram and controller diagram for Xilteor.

2.4 Front Cover Image

The front cover image, which includes our two creatures, is a good indicator of the kinds of poses and deformations that our finished rigs will be capable of (Figure 2.14). The time that we have spent here discussing, planning and preparing these creatures went straight into the successful completion of the rigs that you see

Figure 2.14

The final cover image for this book shows Pheridan and Xilteor in dynamic poses as they battle against each other.

in the final image. All of this work is never wasted, and I really suggest that you spend time in this section really thinking about your own creatures and how you can execute a solid, well-thought-out plan from concept to completion.

2.5 Summary

In this chapter we have looked into the backgrounds and fake lives of our mythical creatures, Pheridan and Xilteor. Both of these creatures live in the same make-believe world and behave, act and move very differently from each other.

We are able to use real-world living creatures as reference, or even other fantastical creations in movies and television to get a better understanding of how these creatures will move. Armed with this information, we've planned out the joints (bones) of these creatures, briefly discussed possible challenges and attributes, and even created controller layouts which we will copy as we move into the 3D rigging process.

It's time to jump into 3ds Max and start our hands-on, practical 3D time. Thing is, we haven't even evaluated the models just yet or even checked out their geometry. We should probably do that first...

3

Rigging Preparation

There are no secrets to success. It is the result of preparation, hard work, and learning from failure.

Colin Powell

Doing some basic checks on the models and scene files that we have been supplied is a little frustrating but very logical. Think about when you purchase a car, motorbike, house or anything where you're going to rely on it and use it for a substantial time. You more than likely want to see it first, try it out, take it for a spin and see if it is for you. Preparing for rigging is exactly that, making sure that what you have to work with is going to be suitable and as enjoyable as it can be to use.

If we fail to prepare correctly, nothing might happen! In fact, everything throughout the rigging process and beyond could go on just fine without any hiccups, issues or problems. If this happens, then I would say congratulations, you've been incredibly lucky! You see, what usually happens is an error at some point. It could be that the scale of the scene is wrong. A dirty node in there slows things down. The scene references a file that no longer exists. And many other complications could arise. The worst of this is that there is a possibility that you will need to redo all of that complicated hard work that you spent hours creating in the first place. A short amount of time spent preparing correctly now is better than spending a lot of time on fixes and redos later.

Throughout this chapter, we will be working on both of the creatures in parallel. The idea of this is that we prepare both of the creatures for rigging and in later chapters we work on one creature at a time to stop any confusion. However, as this chapter is relatively straightforward, we'll be working on the following two files simultaneously:

- 00_CH_Pheridan_START.max
- 00_CH_Xilteor_START.max

3.1 Model and Scene Cleaning

Both of the files that we are using started their life in another software completely. They were then brought into 3ds Max, cleaned up and handed over to me as FBX files – a common kind of file format for 3D. From there I combined them into the same scene, scaled them, added a material and then saved them out into the separate files mentioned above.

What this means is that although we have two working files, they are far from checked and far from being a clean scene. We'll use this chapter to go through various stages in order to get these assets ready for the rigging procedure.

3.1.1 Redundant Object Removal

There may be some additional objects in the scene that really don't belong. These are things that could have been placed temporarily or used in construction and are no longer needed. This is a great point to remove these redundant objects; just be careful that it is not affecting or connected to your scene's geometry or is something that you may need further into the pipeline.

3.1.2 Polygon/Triangle Limits

Now that only the geometry and objects we actually need are left in the scene, this is a good time to check on the amount of polygons and triangles that are left. You can quickly check these by showing statistics in the viewport (hotkey "7"), or grab the *Polygon Counter* utility from the *Utilities* tab.

Polygon/Triangle Counter

```
Hotkey "7"
Or
Viewport Options ([+]) > Configure Viewports… > Statistics
Or
Utilities Tab > More… > Polygon Counter
```

By my counts, here is what the featured creatures have:

- Pheridan
  - Polys: 70,172
  - Tris: 140,302
- Xilteor
  - Polys: 100,972
  - Tris: 110,074

If these readings are too high or don't fit into your pipeline, you have the opportunity now to fix them. Alternatively, if you're working in a professional production, you could send these back to the modeling/asset department so that you can focus on something else until they are within the production parameters.

3.1.3 Topology and Looping Checks

As always, I recommend maintaining a quad topology at all times. Quads are beneficial to everyone in a CG pipeline, enabling predictable surfaces when editing, subdividing and rendering; minimizing texture stretching and allowing for evenly distributed skin weighting and deformations. Triangles are also acceptable and can sometimes happen for a number of reasons such as time constraints or the preservation of polygon counts. So, don't worry if they are present in your models; just place them strategically so that they are hidden or do not affect geometry flow too radically. I'm sure you already know, but if you have a polygon with more than four sides, then fix it up. There's no real excuse to have those things in your geometry.

I'm a big believer that edge flow should loop around the muscles of the creature that we are rigging. This helps dramatically when it comes to achieving realistic deformations, but it is certainly not needed, and is often a luxury that we don't have. In the first *Digital Creature Rigging* book, Belraus (the creature from that book) had muscular-based flowing loops and it was great. This time we've opted for a more common and traditional edge flow that is simply evenly spaced and as four-sided as possible. This will show that great results are possible for both kinds of techniques.

Checking geometry is a relatively simple process, and there are tools available to help you with this, but as we're using no scripts or plugins, we have to analyze the geometry manually – it should only take a short amount of time as you explore.

3.1.4 Units

I'm setting my units as Metric and Meters with my Lighting Units as International. My System Units Setup will be 1 Unit will equal Centimeters. From this point onwards, and for everything associated with these creatures, I won't change these settings at all. Now I know that you already know how important it is to not mess around with these once they are set, but just in case, here's the official text from the Autodesk Knowledge Network:

> Warning: Change the system unit value before you import or create geometry. Do not change the system unit in an existing scene.

Autodesk Knowledge Network

Don't change things once you set it for a project. Never ever!

Unit Setup

```
Customize > Unit Setup…
```

3.1.5 Creature Scale

The size and scale of objects are very important, as changing scales at a later point in a production can cause all sorts of problems. If you have reference geometry or other scenes to work with, you will have a good idea of the sizes that your creatures need to be by default. As we're only working with Pheridan and Xilteor for this book, I like to create a *Biped* which stands at around 6 feet (1.828 meters). This acts as a reference point so I can resize my creature geometry to the size that I think fits best.

If you need to measure something more precisely or accurately, remember that the *Tape Helper* can be of great use. This is particularly useful for measurements where a humanoid character like the *Biped* will not be helpful.

Tape Helper Tool

```
Create Tab > Helpers > Standard > Tape
```

3.1.6 Geometry Coloring

A completely optional step, but I'm very specific with the colors of my geometry. It doesn't make any difference to the operation of 3ds Max or the actual rig, but it helps me greatly while I work. For me, all geometry must be gray and all wireframes must be in **black** (Figure 3.1). Visually, I think this is a lot clearer when colors from tools and controllers start jumping into the viewport!

3.1.7 Geometry Naming

Using the naming conventions that were covered in Chapter 1, I use this time to go in and rename all of the geometry in the scene. Luckily, both Pheridan

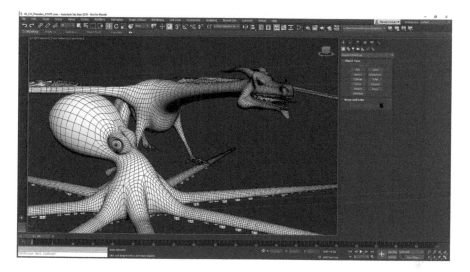

Figure 3.1

I like to view geometry in a single shade of gray with wireframes always displayed in black. This is a personal preference and a completely optional step.

and Xilteor have very few objects, so naming things doesn't take much time at all. Here's the breakdown on the correctly named geometry for both creatures:

- Pheridan
  - CH_pheridan_body_GEO
  - CH_pheridan_eyes_GEO
  - CH_pheridan_beak_GEO
- Xilteor
  - CH_xilteor_body_GEO
  - CH_xilteor_teethGums_GEO
  - CH_xilteor_eyes_GEO
  - CH_xilteor_tongue_GEO

3.1.8 Geometry Hierarchy

With the geometry named correctly, it's time to get it sitting under the same hierarchy. I'm using a *Point Helper* as I usually do, and renaming it to "CH_pheridan_GEO_GRP" for the squid and "CH_xilteor_GEO_GRP" for the dragon. These are placed in the center of the scene, *Position XYZ[0,0,0]*, and I use the *Select and Link* tool to put the geometry into a hierarchy which you can see in the *Schematic View* shown in Figure 3.2.

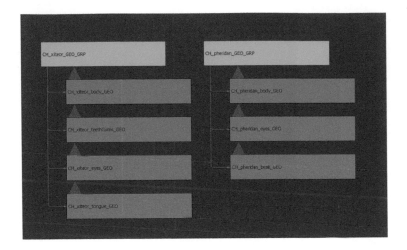

Figure 3.2

The completed geometry hierarchies for Pheridan and Xilteor.

3.1.9 Pivot Points

When the creature's geometry is in the position that I want it to be before rigging, which is usually close to the center of the scene, I like to change the pivot points. I do this for each object, moving the pivots to the center of the scene and resetting them to world space.

3.1.10 Resetting XForms

Make sure to make a copy of your file before doing this next step. I've had some crazy things happen when resetting transforms on objects, so it's better to be safe than sorry. Once you have a duplicate of your file as a backup, head on over to the *Utilities Panel* and use that *Reset XForm* button.

Reset XForms

```
[Select Geometry] Utilities Panel > Reset XForm > Reset
Selected
```

Remember to convert your geometry back to *Editable Poly* in order to collapse the *Modifier Stack* and leave the geometry as clean as possible.

Convert to Editable Poly

```
[Select Geometry] Right-Click > Convert To: > Convert to
Editable Poly
```

3.1.11 Freeze Transformations

We can finish up the model cleaning by freezing the transformations of the objects. By doing this, we set the positional, rotational and scale values to zero, and we should do this for all objects in the scene.

Freeze Transformations

```
[Select Geometry] Alt and Right-Click > Freeze Transform >
Click "Yes" in the newly opened window
```

3.1.12 Save Selected

Save out the creatures by using the *Save Selected* method instead of the usual *Save* or *Save As* options. This will allow you to specifically pick the objects that you want to save and drop anything else in the scene that we may have missed while we were clearing everything out and making things as clean as possible.

Save Selected Method

```
[Select Objects] File > Save Select…
```

Once you've saved this new file, remember to open it first before jumping on to the next step!

3.2 Display Layers

Since the first *Digital Creature Rigging* book, not much has changed for the *Display Layers*. Everything is still there, and the only addition is one layer that contains deformation objects (see Table 3.1).

This is still my preferred method for setting up layers that control what can be seen in our scenes. If you're working in a production, you may have to fit your workflows into an already existing style, but this should give you a good idea of how things can be split into logical and clear categories.

3.3 Save for Rigging

That's pretty much everything. Hit that *Save* button and you will have yourself a ready-to-rig file that's ready for a production. Be sure to bundle your files up appropriately and it's probably good to make a duplicate and save them somewhere as a backup and for archiving (Figure 3.3).

Table 3.1 Display Layers

Layer	Description
0 (Default)	Automatically created by 3ds Max.
ANIM	Used for animation-specific data.
BS	BS stands for "Blendshapes," a term used in Autodesk Maya which refers directly to Morph Targets in 3ds Max. I know, I should probably change this, but I'm so used to it...
CAM	Cameras! Any and all kinds of them go in here.
CTRL	Short for "controls" or "controllers." This is where we will put the animatable controls of our rigs.
DATA	Nodes which hold attributes or specific data information are stored in this layer.
DEFORM	Deformation nodes sit in this layer.
FX	Effects objects and emitters go in here.
GEO	All geometry should be placed into this layer.
LI	Lights used to illuminate the scene and its objects reside in here.
MSCLE	Muscles! Although these are technically deformation nodes, we keep this separate so that they are easier to find, as things can often become complicated in technical rigs.
RIG	All rigging-related nodes that don't fit into the other layers should be found in this layer.
SKEL	This is the closet for all of your skeletons!
WIP	This is the "work in progress" layer. It's here where we will be storing everything as we develop things, before moving completed work into the other layers.

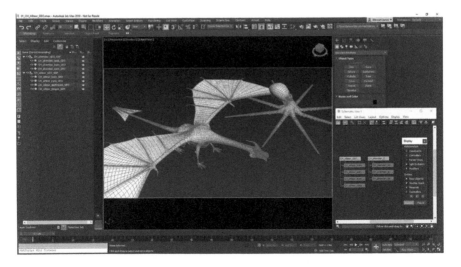

Figure 3.3

Both creatures are clean and ready for rigging to begin.

3.4 Summary

The steps we took here were certainly not difficult; in fact, for someone who is accustomed to the operations of 3ds Max, this chapter will have breezed on by and that's a good thing. This chapter is not here to trip you up, it is here to allow you to do basic rigging preparations as quickly and as easily as possible.

With this stage complete, we can move ahead and start the rigging process for each of the creatures. Of course, this chapter covered the rigging preparations process just once, but the idea is that you replicate the same procedures for both of the creatures. However, from here on out we'll be working through each of the rigging stages separately for the two creatures. Don't worry, we'll bring these two titans back together at the end so that they can take part in that epic battle that you see on the front cover of this book!

We end this chapter with the following two files to work on going forward:

- 00_CH_Pheridan_GEO.max
- 00_CH_Xilteor_GEO.max

4

Pheridan

Base Rig

Squid experts have been debating for some time about whether the giant squid is a passive predator that just floats around in the water and waits to bump into something. I was never one to imagine it to be passive.

Edith Widder

We can now dive into the rigging process by metaphorically plunging into the depths of the ocean as we start our journey with the creation of an aquatic rig for the giant squid, Pheridan. This eight-limbed creature has a number of technical challenges which we must overcome in order to deliver a successful creature rig that can be used in a number of different ways.

At this stage in the development of the rig, we will focus on the core structures and foundations which we will build upon as we go forward. This means that we need to work cleanly and logically in order to give a solid framework to work from. We'll be looking into the core hierarchy of the rig, adding the existing geometry to it, creating joints/bones, creating a way to check the creature's location, adding in some basic skinning deformations, saving out animation for skin testing and even adding in the controllers. All of this will be done during this phase of the rig's development, and all taken care of in this chapter.

We will be working from the following file during this chapter:

- 01_CH_Pheridan_GEO.max

4.1 Core Hierarchical Structure

To start things off, we need to create a *ROOT* node which will be used as the most upper node in the creature's hierarchy... The, err, root of everything, if you will. Now, I'm a huge fan of using an *ExposeTM Helper* object for this, but it's important to be aware that this object in particular has issues when being exported and imported into real-time engines like Unity or Unreal. It's a simple fix to switch out the *ExposeTM* for a *Point Helper* at a later point, but if you're specifically working with real-time engines, it might make more sense to use that *Point Helper* now rather than later. Again, I'll be using the *ExposeTM Helper* right now, but I'll leave it up to you decide which *Helper* object makes more sense for you to be using from the beginning. So, create your *ROOT* node and place it at the center of the scene, *XYZ[0,0,0]*.

Creating the Root Node

1. Create an *ExposeTM* Helper.
   ```
   Create Tab > Helpers > Standard > ExposeTm
   ```
2. Change its appearance to however you like it. I prefer an *Axis Tripod*, *Center Marker* and *Cube*.
3. Move the object to the center of the scene, *XYZ[0,0,0]*.

Rename your *ROOT* node correctly using the naming conventions, which will give you something like *CH_pheridan_ROOT* if you're following along and rigging the Pheridan creature with me. Next up is the need to create a number of nodes which will be used to group together various rig components. I'll be using *Point Helpers* for all of the group nodes, and they will all sit in the center of the scenes at *XYZ[0,0,0]*. We already have a *CH_pheridan_GEO_GRP* in our scene already, so we don't need to worry about creating another one. To create the other objects, it is the same procedure as creating the *ROOT* node, so I'll let you jump in and create the following *Point Helper* objects in your scene:

- CH_pheridan_CTRL_GRP
- CH_pheridan_RIG_GRP
- CH_pheridan_SKEL_GRP
- CH_pheridan_WIP

---

4. Pheridan: Base Rig

With these nodes created, all we need to do is use the *Schematic View* or other tools to *Select and Link* these nodes into one cohesive hierarchy, which should look just like this (Figure 4.1):

- CH_pheridan_ROOT
  - CH_pheridan_CTRL_GRP
  - CH_pheridan_GEO_GRP
    - [Geometry Objects]
  - CH_pheridan_RIG_GRP
  - CH_pheridan_SKEL_GRP
  - CH_pheridan_WIP

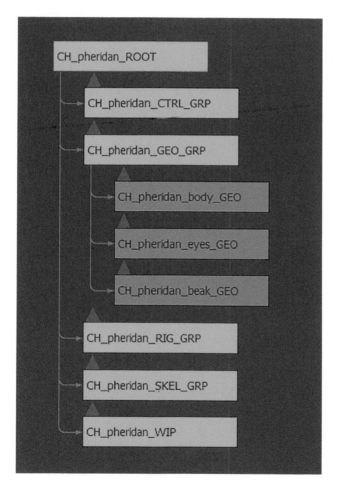

Figure 4.1

Pheridan's completed base hierarchy.

4.2 Bone Creation and Placement

Before we place any of the *Bones* for our creature, I have to mention that I'm really terrible for using the term *Joints* instead of *Bones*. This stems from using both 3ds Max and Maya, as *Bones* are named *Joints* in Maya. They technically do the same thing and behave in similar ways, but you may notice the term *Joints* used instead of *Bones* throughout this text and other texts. Please just be aware that they mean the same thing; it's nothing fancy or special, just a different label for them.

Creating *Bones* in 3ds Max is a simple process and we can either choose to build them directly from the *Systems Button* found on the *Create* tab or from the *Bone Tools* rollout. As both ways create the same kinds of *Bones*, it doesn't matter which way you choose to create them. However, the *Bone Tools* rollout offers a number of other options not available from the *Systems* button, so I prefer opening that rollout most of the time (Figure 4.2).

Creating Bones

```
Create Tab > Systems Button > Standard > Bones
Or
Animation Menu > Bone Tools… > Create Bones
```

Okay, with all of that said, let's jump into the creation of the *Bones* for Pheridan.

4.2.1 Center of Gravity

As with every creature, human or even nonorganic rig, I like to start with the *Bone* that will be placed at the center of gravity, also known as COG. This *Center Of Gravity Bone* is usually at the hips for a human or biped, often the same for four-legged animals (quadrupeds) or sometimes at the chest. In order to make sure I'll be placing this *Bone* in the correct location, I keep in mind a simple question that is often very helpful:

Where does the movement originate from on this creature?

The answer to this question is more often than not the location of the *COG*. For our Pheridan creature, I imagine the *COG* to be situated somewhere in the center of the torso area, and I come to this conclusion through a mixture of both estimation (guessing) and the viewing of reference videos on how a squid moves and swims. Oh, and the *COG* for Pheridan is a simple one-*Bone* chain, as shown in Figure 4.3.

4.2.2 Torso and Head

Working up from the *COG*, we can build a chain of *Bones* to give us the basic structure for the torso and head of Pheridan. We could just create the *Bones* arbitrarily for this section and it would work just great, but I'd like to use a *Line* to help me visualize where the *Bones* will be placed first. This can be a simple two-vertex *Line* running from the *COG* to the back/top of the head (Figure 4.4).

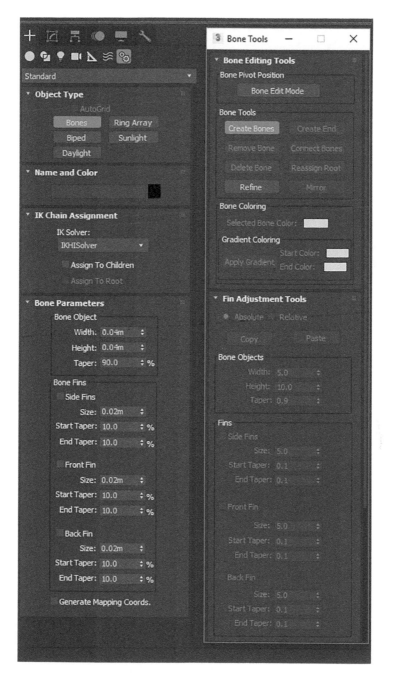

Figure 4.2

The *Bone Tools* rollout and *Systems* button allow us to create *Bones*, but some options are missing from the *Systems* tab.

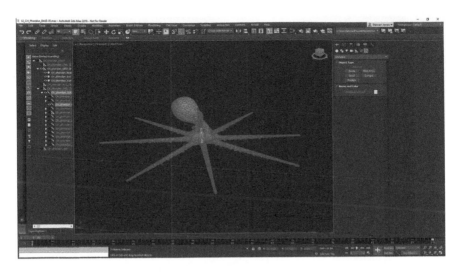

Figure 4.3

The *COG Bone* correctly placed for Pheridan.

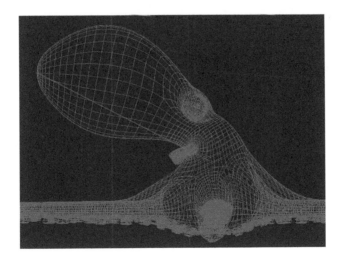

Figure 4.4

A simple two-vertex *Line* added from the *COG* to the back/top of Pheridan's head.

With the *Line* in place, we can convert both vertices into *Bezier* handles so that we can edit and adapt the shape of the *Line* so that it fits to the center of the geometry better. Once the shape of the *Line* is more suitable, we can easily add a *Normalize Spline* modifier which will automatically add extra vertices. Changing the *Max Knots* option on this modifier allows us to specify the maximum number of vertices we will have on the *Line*. I'm setting this number to *15*.

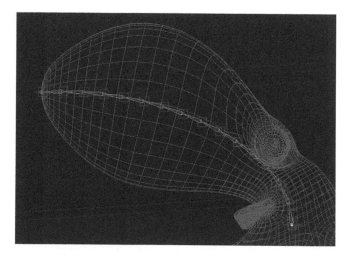

Figure 4.5

The adapted *Line* using *Bezier* handles, a *Normalize Spine* modifier and *Point Helpers* automatically created by using a *Spline IK Control* modifier. The *Bones* have been added by snapping to the *Point Helper's* pivots.

Now that we've done a little bit of setup and adjustments to the *Line*, we can easily add a *Spline IK Control* modifier and press the *Create Helpers* button. This adds a number of *Point Helpers* to the *Line* to which we can snap the *Bones* of the torso and head (Figure 4.5).

Creating, Editing, Rebuilding and Controlling Splines

1. Create a *Line*.
   ```
   Create Tab > Shapes > Splines > Line
   ```
2. Select the vertices and convert them to *Bezier* (if they aren't already).
   ```
   [Select Line] > Modify Tab > Selection > Vertex
   ```
3. Edit the *Bezier handles* to the desired shape.
   ```
   [Select vertex] > Right-click > Tools 1 > Bezier
   ```
4. Add a *Normalize Spline* modifier and edit the *Max Knots* option to change the total number of newly created vertices.
   ```
   [Select Line] > Modify Tab > Modifier List > Normalize
   Spline
   ```
5. Add a *SplineIK Control* modifier.
   ```
   [Select Line] > Modify Tab > Modifier List > SplineIK
   Control
   ```
6. Click the *Create Helpers* button to automatically create *Point Helpers* positioned at the vertices which can actually be used to control the *Line*.

Once those *Bones* are in place, we can simply delete the *Line* and the extra *Point Helpers* that were created so that our scene is clean once more. We can then move onto the limbs.

4.2.3 Tentacles (Limbs)

Using the exact same method we did for the torso and head, we can create the *Bones* for one of the tentacles of the squid. I'm not making any changes at all to the setup here, with the exception that I'm starting with a three-vertex *Line* to better enable me to trace the inside of the tentacle. From there it's just the same: edit the *Bezier* handles, add a *Normalize Spline* modifier with *15 Max Knots*, then a *SplineIK Control* modifier with the created *Point Helpers* dictating the *pivot point* locations for each of the *Bones* that needs to be created (Figure 4.6).

Figure 4.6

A pretty much identical setup to the torso and head is used for one of the tentacles (limbs) of Pheridan.

With the *Bones* for the limb in place, we can delete the setup to clean things up a little. We can now create another *Point Helper* and position this at the center of the scene, *XYZ[0,0,0]*. With that in place, use the *Select and Link* tool, or another similar tool, to connect the uppermost limb *Bone* to it. This should mean that when the *Point Helper* is transformed, the *Bones* will follow along with it, as they are in the same hierarchy.

4. Pheridan: Base Rig

It's now time to create the *Bones* for the remaining tentacles. To do this, we need to *duplicate* the setup we have just created a total of seven more times. This will give us eight limbs which we can position in the center of the scene and rotate so that the *Bone* chains all fit into their respective limbs just like in Figure 4.7.

Figure 4.7

All the *Bone* chains have been repositioned so that they fit within the geometry at each of the tentacles.

You may notice that not all of the tentacles are created equally; I mean we wouldn't want it to be too easy, right?! Don't worry, though; this setup will require you to rotate the *Bone* chains at uneven rotations, but we'll be using the same kinds of controls and rigging for each of them. Oh, and some tentacles are longer or shorter than others. Again, no need to worry – there's no need to fix these up, we're just going to roll with it!

4.2.4 Exhausts

A simple two-*Bone* chain can be used for both of the exhausts. I've simply *mirrored* one side to the other and manually positioned them to fit. If you're working on the Pheridan model with me, you'll notice that the geometry is not exactly the same on either side. So, just like with the limbs, the *Bones* for the exhausts may not fit both sides perfectly, but we'll keep the same setup for both to make the rigging process a little faster.

4.2.5 Beak

Underneath the creature is its beak. I'm using a single *Bone* chain for both the front and back of the beak. When placed, these cross, making a kind of an "X" visually, and should be more than enough to control this area (Figure 4.8).

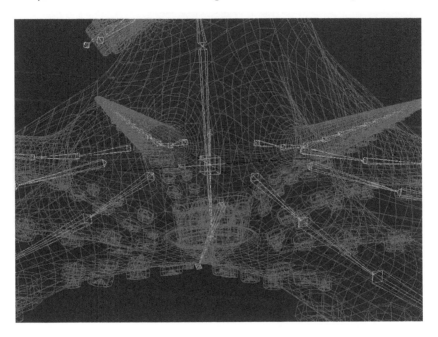

Figure 4.8

The beak is the easiest setup and only requires one *Bone* for each section.

4.3 Building the Skeletal Hierarchy

Before we build the skeletal hierarchy, it's that time where we should really start naming everything so that we know what all of these *Bone* chains are. As always, I'm using the naming conventions we set out in Chapter 1 and I'll be using the *Schematic View* in order to *Select and Link* the *Bones* into one single hierarchy, just like in Figure 4.9. I won't go into all of the exact naming I'm using for each of the *Bones*, as this would not only be extremely tedious, but is not relevant or needed in order to follow along with this book. If you really must know, open up the file mentioned at the end of this chapter and check everything out for yourself.

With everything named correctly, we can go ahead and start linking everything together. In particular, I'm linking the following objects to for one skeletal hierarchy:

- Torso to the COG.
- Limbs to the COG.

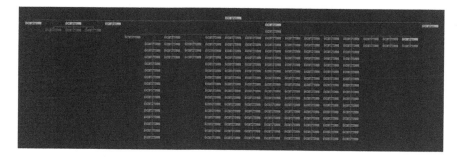

Figure 4.9

The correctly named and linked hierarchy for Pheridan.

- Beak to the COG.
- Exhaust to the Torso.

Add this skeletal hierarchy under *CH_pheridan_SKEL_GRP*, and we can move on to checking the *Local Rotation Axis* (LRA) of the *Bones*.

4.3.1 Local Rotation Axis

The *Local Rotation Axis* for created *Bones* in 3ds Max is often an overlooked and forgotten step that can make a huge difference to the behavior of our rigs. This is mostly due to the fact that *LRAs* are not a well-documented feature of this software in comparison to other 3D applications. In fact, displaying a *Bones's* LRA in 3ds Max requires some kind of script or plugin. Now, writing a script to show these *LRAs* is not too technically challenging, but it's kind of annoying that this is not a built-in feature already. Additionally, as this book uses no extra third-party plugins or scripts, we have to make do with what 3ds Max provides us with... And out of the box, that equals nothing for *LRA* viewing! Not a great start.

Accessing and Editing the Local Rotation Axis of a Bone

1. Change the *Rotate* tool to rotate in *Local* mode.
   ```
   Main Toolbar > Select and Rotate (E) > Reference
   Coordinate System > Local
   ```
2. Turn on *Bone Edit Mode* in the *Bone Tools* rollout.
   ```
   Animation Menu > Bone Tools... > Bone Edit Mode
   ```
3. Rotate the *Bone* on its *twisting axis*.
4. Turn off Bone Edit Mode.
   ```
   Animation Menu > Bone Tools... > Bone Edit Mode
   ```
5. Freeze *Transformation* on the edited *Bone* to reset it.
   ```
   [Select Bone] > Alt & Right-Click > Freeze Transforms >
   Popup Menu > Yes
   ```

Luckily, we can rely on the standard *rotate* tool and switching the *rotation mode* to *local*. With that set, we can *Freeze Transformations* on all of the *Bones* in the skeleton, then manually check each *Bone* to see how it rotates. If any behave in an undesirable fashion, then it's a case of opening the *Bone Tools* rollout, turning on the *Bone Edit Mode* and rotating the troublesome *Bones* on their *twisting axis*, which is usually the *X Rotation*. When you're happy with the results, simply *Freeze Transforms* on those *Bones* once more and the skeleton will behave as required.

4.3.2 Location Information Data Node

If you're working in a real-time engine or are doing some complex morphing to the geometry, you may need to access the positional information for this creature rig. In order to make this easy to access, I usually add a *Location Information Data Node*, which is a quick and easy setup.

This data node needs to be able to send positional ground-plane data to some sort of additional system, this system obviously changes depending on your specific needs. The information that this node has includes forward and backwards motion and well as side-to-side movement. This information translates to *X* and *Y* position information in 3ds Max, as the *Z-axis* represents the vertical axis (up and down). Figure 4.10 shows the finished setup for Pheridan.

By using a trusty *Point Helper* which is aligned to the creature's *COG* in *X* and *Y*, then linked to the *COG Bone*, we're pretty much done with the setup.

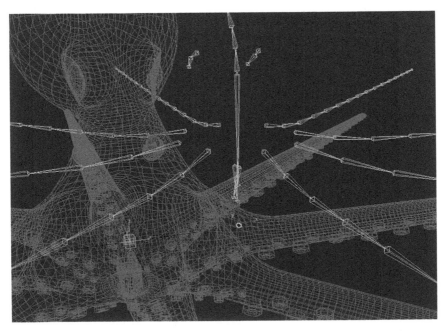

Figure 4.10

The *Location Data Information Node* added to the Pheridan rig.

4. Pheridan: Base Rig

From there we can simply disable the *Move Z Inherit Lock* and it's done. I usually include an additional *Bone* which is connected as both a visual representation and the actual node, which I use to output the ground-plane positional data. By adding this *Bone*, it also gives some sort of *Pivot Point* reference information on the ground = plane level of the creature rig and scene.

Location Data Information Node Creation

1. Create a *Point Helper* and position it at the center of the scene, *XYZ [0,0,0]*.
   ```
   Create Tab > Helpers > Standard > Point Helper
   ```
2. Align the *Pivot Point* only to the *COG* of the creature.
   ```
   [Select Point Helper] > Hierarchy Tab > Pivot > Affect
   Pivot Only
   Align Tool > COG > XYZ Potion > Pivot Point to Pivot
   Point > OK
   Turn off Affect Pivot Only
   ```
3. Link the *Point Helper* to the creature's *COG*.
   ```
   [Select Point Helper] > Main Toolbar > Select and Link
   ```
4. Lock the Move, Rotate and Scale of the Point Helper.
   ```
   [Select Point Helper] > Hierarchy Tab > Link Info >
   Locks > Move, Rotate, Scale XYZ
   ```
5. Turn off all *Inherits* except for the *Move X* and *Move Y* (Figure 4.11).
   ```
   [Select Point Helper] > Hierarchy Tab > Link Info >
   Inherit > Move XY (selected only
   ```
6. Create a single *Bone* at the location of the *Point Helper* and link it together.
   ```
   Animation Menu > Bone Tools… > Create Bones
   ```

I'm ending the creation of this node by correctly renaming the *Point Helper* and *Bone*… As always!

4.4 Base Skinning

The goal of skinning our creature at such an early stage is to highlight any possible issues with our *Bone* placement, check for any problems with the geometry and get a smooth-looking skinning deformation so that we have something to build upon later. This stage was covered in detail in the first book, *Digital Creature Rigging: The Art and Science of CG Creature Setup in 3ds Max* (Jones, 2012), so we'll skip over the real basics of the skinning process this time around. However, a quick refresh on this stage isn't going to be a bad thing, so here's how it works:

- We start by adding a rough, very blocky skinning to the geometry by assigning *100% weighting* to each *Bone*.
- Use the *Mirror Skin* tools if possible.
- We then remove any *Zero Weights* from the *Skin* modifier.

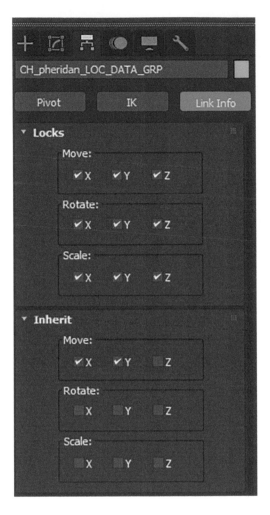

Figure 4.11

The *Locks* and *Inherits* set correctly for the *Location Data Information Node.*

- From there, it's time to change the *Bone Affect Limit* if you need to (important for real-time engines).
- Finally, we're able to smooth out the skinning data by adding blended weights in steps of 0%, 10%, 25%, 50%, 75%, 90% and 100%.

Let's see how this works out for our Pheridan creature by adding a *Skin* modifier to its main geometry and attaching all of the *Bones* to that modifier. For the eyes of this creature, I'm only adding the torso *Bones*, as these are the only *Bones* that need to affect this geometry at the moment. Additionally, the beak area only has the beak *Bones* attached to it, as no other *Bones* are needed.

As usual, 3ds Max adds its best-guess skinning information as we add *Bone* to the *Skin* modifier, and it does an okay job of estimating the desired deformations. However, I'm pretty controlling over this step, so I blast out all of that data and replace it with 100% weighting to the *COG*. From there I can work on each *Bone* and assign "blocked weighting" to the specific vertices I want it to affect. It's time consuming but I find that it gives the best results and makes for a fun-looking multicolored squid at this point (Figure 4.12).

Figure 4.12

With blocked weighting added to Pheridan, he becomes a crazy multicolored squid.

If we go ahead and rotate any of the *Bones*, we now have some kind of basic deformations happening. They are not particularly pretty at this point, but they are practical. I also didn't mirror any skinning information for this creature as it does not have identical geometry on each side. So, before we jump in and smooth out this skinning data, I like to go ahead and *Remove Zero Weights* and then edit the *Bone Affect Limit* to a number that is suitable for the production that I'm currently working on.

Removing Zero Weights

1. With the *Skin* modifier enabled, turn on the *Vertices* option and then select all of the vertices on the model.
   ```
   [Select Geometry] > Modify Tab > Skin > Edit Envelopes
   > Vertices > [Select all vertices]
   ```
2. Head to the *Advanced Parameters* rollout and click the *Remove Zero Weights* button.
   ```
   [With vertices selected] > Advanced Parameters > Remove
   Zero Weights
   ```

Although for this book I could leave this option alone, I'm going to set the *Bone Affect Limit* to 4 which is in line with real-time engines at the time of writing this.

Changing the Bone Affect Limit

It's important to know what the *Bone Affect Limit* number should be for the production that you are working on. If you're unsure, setting this attribute to *4* is a good guess, as this is a common parameter setting for many real-time engines.
```
[Select Geometry] > Modify Tab > Skin > Advanced
Parameters > Bone Affect Limit > (Change to desired
number. Default is 20)
```

4.4.1 Smooth Skinning

Our task is to now improve the blocking we did and convert things into a smoother-looking deformation. We do this by blending weights together, and although it's a relatively straightforward task, it can take a long time to complete. Figure 4.13 shows the method I use as I tackle this challenge.

Go and grab a beverage, put on some music and let's get on with this section…

I'm once again working out from the *COG* of the Pheridan creature in a relatively logical fashion. I work upwards through the torso, blending what I can as a tube; difficulties arise around the eye sockets for the creature and they require some creative thinking to get them to deform as you would expect them to. It's then a case of doing the same thing with the exhausts and making sure that the

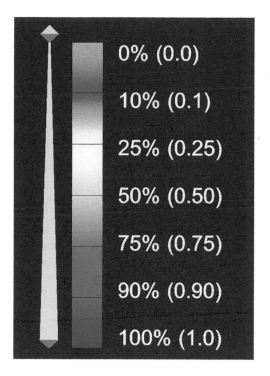

Figure 4.13

This is a visual representation of the basic method I use for attaining a great-looking smooth skin deformation.

torso, head and exhausts all work together correctly. From there it's those eight limbs to take care of and finally the beak and that area underneath the creature. Then you're done with skinning, for now.

Just before we move on, I just want to mention that although this section of this book is relatively small, the actual task of doing this is huge. I mean I've actually spent more time in the skinning of this creature than I have in any of the other previous sections combined. It's crazy to think that this relatively short description of the tasks covers the crazy amount of work that skinning takes. I know you already know all of this, but I thought it was a funny thing to mention as I sit here writing this and skinning Pheridan at the same time. Okay, back to it!

Hours later…

4.4.2 Save Skinning Data

If you get to this point, congratulations. The actual skinning of the creature can be a long and tedious process, and the Pheridan geometry, although fantastic, is not the easiest to skin – it may not be extremely complicated, but it is somewhat tedious.

I've taken the smooth skinning of this creature to a pretty good point overall. I wouldn't call this finished, but it is good enough to save and move on to other things. I'm obviously making a conscious decision to do this, as I know that I will revisit the skin weights as I move into the setup of the deformation rig.

All right, just so we make sure that we don't lose all of this progress, it's a good point to save out the skinning data. There are three ways to do this, which are

- Save as a new file.
- Use the *Skin Utilities* to extract a skin data file.
- Use the *Skin* modifier to extract a skin data file.

I'll leave the choice up to you as to which method or methods you would like to use.

4.5 Bone Shaping

This is a completely optional step, but can look pretty great as a visual representation of the creature. It also acts as stand-in geometry, removing the need to display soft-surface deformations in our viewports, which requires very little processing power from our computer systems – helpful if we are working on a rig that is behaving slowly for whatever reasons.

Reshaping Bones

1. Add an *Edit Poly* modifier to a *Bone*.
   `[Select Bone] > Modify Tab > Modifier List > Edit Poly`
2. Use the tools on the *Edit Poly* modifier to adjust the *Bone*'s shape.
3. You can copy and paste modifiers from one *Bone* to another if you need to and then use a *Mirror* modifier to flip the edited shape around as you need to.

Reshaping *Bones* is a simple case of adding an *Edit Poly* modifier to a *Bone* and then using common modeling tools to edit the shape of it. To transfer these edits to the opposite side of our creature, it's a simple case of copying and pasting the modifier from one to another. Then add a *Mirror* modifier and adjust those parameters in order for it to fit correctly. I'm opting not to do this for Pheridan, but the choice is there if you'd like to.

4.6 Range of Motion File

A range of motion (ROM) file is nothing more than an animation file which, when applied to a creature, shows the full range of motion that is acceptable for it. ROM files are not full of beautiful animations, though; actually, they are far from it. At their core, these files are nothing more than extreme poses linearly animated into and out of.

Really, there's nothing special here, just pose after crazy pose stress-testing the creature to its limits. If you're working in a production, it's probably a good idea to get an animator to create these files; however, this may not be an option, as people are often busy, or it may be all up to you. But, that's no problem; like I said, these are not pretty animations, just raw movements, pose to pose, position to position.

You may be thinking that there is no rig for this creature yet, and you'd be right, there isn't! So, no matter who is going to create the ROM file, they need to be comfortable animating directly on the *Bones*, or it's even better if they (or you) are able to create fast-and-dirty temporary rigs in order to get into the positions that the creature will need.

Once you have the ROM file and it shows a dynamic range of positions, it's time to save it out. Again, there are a few options for doing this, and I'm giving you the freedom to choose which option or options you prefer to use:

- Save out a new file.
- Save out an FBX animation file.
- Bake down the trajectories and save an animation file.

4.7 Motion Set List

Real-time engines usually have some kind of blend trees, blend graphs or motion-blending tools specifically used to give a visual representation of how animations work together. More recently, these kinds of systems are being used in prerendered environments in things like crowd simulations or even real-time engines used as previsualization and even through to the final image. Whatever your use is for this kind of technology, this might be the perfect time to start thinking about how animations are going to blend together.

For instance, a human character standing idle. If we want it to walk and then run, there are two transitions which need to be built for this. The first transition is from the idle to the walk, the second from the walk to the run. If we want that character to go back to idle, we need to add another transition as it slows down from the run into the idle animations. In these situations, we can animate the various stages and animate the transitions as well, but we could let the blending system take care of that for us.

Now, going into the specifics of these systems is way out of the scope of this book, and honestly, it's just not our focus right now. But, if your production or project requires you to use these kinds of systems, I suggest taking some time to work out a few of these things right now. It might save you a few headaches or head-scratching moments later on.

4.8 Controller Creation

Using the planning images that were made during Chapter 2, "The Creatures," we can now adapt those controller diagrams and actually create the controllers in 3D. There are many options for the kinds of controls that can be used in a creature rig, but my personal preference is to use *Shapes* made from *Splines*. I like using these for a number of reasons; first, they are visually appealing and can be shaped and molded into many various forms which can look great on our rigs. Second, they are easy to create and perform quickly in the viewports. Last, they are self explanatory for others using our rigs, and they look like controllers, act like controllers and work great as controllers!

Creating Controllers Using Shapes (Splines)

1. Create a *Spline* object of any kind.
   `Create Tab > Shapes > Splines > (Multiple Options)`
2. You can convert created *Shapes* into *Editable Splines* and combine them using the *Attach* button or edit them using sub-object modes. The possibilities are as endless as our imaginations!

All that's left to do is correctly color those controllers using our previously mentioned color conventions outlined in Chapter 1, "Introduction," and then we can end this chapter with a completed *Base Rig*. However, I'm going against the color conventions at this point and will color all of my controllers in a boring gray tone. I'll be changing these colors to the correct colors as we work our way through the animation rig, but for now I want to keep things as visually neutral as possible, just like in Figure 4.14.

Figure 4.14

Pheridan and all of the controllers finish out this chapter.

4. Pheridan: Base Rig

4.9 Summary

We created a core hierarchy for our creature, placed and positioned the *Bones* of the skeleton and created smooth-skin deformations that will all serve as the base rig of this creature for the upcoming sections. The solid foundations that we have built here will be a part of this creature for all other areas of its development, way past the rigging stages.

Pheridan's base rig is now complete and ready to move into the animation rig phase. Things are going to get tricky and complicated from this point out, but the tasks that we'll be doing to solve the rigging challenge for this creature are fun and exciting. Let's swim on over and forgive my bad puns!

Reference

Jones, S. 2012. *Digital Creature Rigging: The Art and Science of CG Creature Setup in 3ds Max*. Boca Raton, FL: CRC Press.

5

Pheridan

Animation Rig

I'd like to see the giant squid. Nobody has ever seen one. I could tell you people who have spent thousands and thousands of pounds trying to see giant squid. I mean, we know they exist because we have seen dead ones. But I have never seen a living one. Nor has anybody else.

David Attenborough

The second layer of our multilayered rigging approach is the animation rig and this, combined with the deformation rig, forms the core complexities of the rigging process. It is where we give specific and deliberate controls over our creatures using methods and techniques that aim to make interaction with our creatures as easy as possible. The trouble is that these deceptively simple controls often require us to accomplish technically challenging feats but offer them to the end user in a way that removes that complexity from their interactions. If we didn't have to do this, a rig would be nothing more than a base rig with some fancy deformers that make the geometry move, stick and slide correctly.

At the core of the animation rig, our aim is to provide an interface with which to directly control and manipulate our creatures. These controls take the most punishment from the users of the rigs we create, so it's important that things work as expected at all times. It is this layer where we make sure our rig can perform at 80% or 90% of what will be needed for this creature's movements.

We'll be using the research we did during Chapter 2, "The Creatures," in order to create controls that will allow us to intuitively manipulate our creature through the movements and positions we already envisioned. Additionally, any ROM files we created will be very important for us to make sure our interfaces allow users of the rig to achieve the correct positions, and this will become even more important as we move past this stage – but, let's think about that later.

For now, we need to create our animation rig, and we will be working from the following file during this chapter:

- 02_CH_Pheridan_BASE.max

5.1 The Connections

We've spoken a lot about the layered system that we're using in our approach to rigging this creature, and we haven't really put things into practice just yet, but now would be a good time to start. You see, many rigs apply various techniques and solutions directly to the base rig, removing the need for additional layers and complexities which we inevitably build into a multilayered approach. It also takes a lot more time to rig something with this multilayered approach, so it can be challenging to incorporate into time-critical rigging builds.

So, why do we do things the hard way? Well, I can tell you that not using multiple layers in your rigging approach is a perfectly valid method of doing things. However, by doing this, you increase the possibility of serious complications arising as your rig works through a production pipeline and out of the realms of rigging and into other departments. Things like the flipping of *Bones*, random errors on exporting, nonclean hierarchies and double transformations can become a very unwanted occurrence in any rig, but removing these problems from rigs which aren't built on multiple layers can be a nightmare of epic proportions. Oh, and double transformations are when an object transforms more than what we intend it to.

Splitting a rig into multiple layers allows us to focus on one section at a time and then combine layers together to create the final rig (Figure 5.1). It also means that if problems do pop up, we can confine them to just one layer, meaning that if we need to scrap a whole layer, the rest of the rig stays intact. If we built this on just one layer, we may have to restart the rigging process from the very beginning, throwing away hours and hours of hard work.

However, I'm very familiar with the pressures of working in productions and to strict and rigid deadlines where taking the best approach is not always an option. When creating Belraus for the first *Digital Creature Rigging* book, there was the luxury of being able to have the time and freedom to apply all of these various layers and complexities to the rig. This time I want to do things in a more fluid way, and I'll be using a mixture of techniques to create the rigs in this book. This means that although the best choice would be to work on a layered-rigging

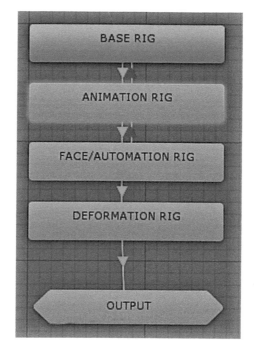

Figure 5.1

The connections between rigs that use the multilayered rigging approach.

approach, we're not going to do that and we're going to just build everything in a more fluid manner. Hopefully this will not only demonstrate that there are always multiple ways to do things but also show that we can make things work no matter the limitations and pressures pushing against us.

5.2 Broken Hierarchies

A single skeleton structure, just like the one we have in Pheridan's base rig, is perfect for sending into real-time engines and crowd simulation software. We have to be careful with a few things like the amount of *Bones* that have a deformation effect over each vertex, how many *Bones* are in the skeleton and if we're using move, rotation and scale data for the animation. But generally, a single skeleton hierarchical structure is needed.

Broken hierarchies are commonplace in film and television rigs where they aren't constrained by technology quite as much. A broken hierarchy refers to a rig with a hierarchical structure that is not directly linked together. Now all of these separate hierarchies live under the *ROOT* node in some way, but a hierarchy created for the head of a creature will not be directly linked (in terms of hierarchical structure) to the neck, which would be the obvious choice of places to link it to. Now that's not to say it won't be connected in some way such as constraints, wire parameters or other methods, but it won't be directly linked in the hierarchy.

We create these broken hierarchies for a number of different reasons, the most important being that we can create modular components that can be attached, unattached and reattached as we need them to be. It also allows us to duplicate various sections of components and hierarchies for other areas of the rig that may need a similar kind of setup. This is extremely helpful, to say the least.

For both Pheridan and Xilteor, we will be keeping the single skeleton hierarchy completely intact for the base rig, allowing these creatures to be easily exported out into various other engines so they can be used for many different productions. When it comes to the animation rig, we will be using broken hierarchies everywhere and as this layer sits on top of the base rig, we get the best of both worlds – a solid, structurally sound single skeleton hierarchy and the flexibility and practicality of a broken hierarchy.

5.3 The Animation Rig

This is where things get real! Okay, not literally real, as we're working in a 3D application, but as real as we can possibly get... The work is real, if nothing else.

For each section of the creature, we will break things down into separate sections and work through them systematically. This will allow us to really focus on the specifics of every single element that makes up the creature's rig. It also lets us work through things in a step-by-step manner where we can dive into each of the complex areas putting things together as we go and eventually wrapping things up into a finished animation rig.

Oh, and here's the coolest part. During the *Digital Creature Rigging: The Art and Science of CG Creature Setup in 3ds Max* book, we started by duplicating the base rig skeleton and using that to build our animation rig. This time, we're going to be using a crazy amount of *Point Helpers* instead.

Here we go…

5.3.1 Center of Gravity

The most important part of our creature is the *COG*, as this is where all of its movement radiates from, and for our squid, this is in the lower-central section. Thing is, this might be the most important part, but it is one of the easiest to rig. All we need to do is add a *Point Helper* to the scene and *align* it to the *COG*; this is going to be what our controller actually controls, and the *COG* is going to be controlled by the *Point Helper* via a *Link Constraint* (Figure 5.2), which is part of the *Transform Controllers*. Color that COG control so that we know that the COG setup is complete.

I'll mention this only once from here on out, but remember to name everything that you create and use in the rig. We've got the naming conventions to follow, so just make sure you're being consistent. That's it. Really, that's all there is to it.

The COG Setup

1. Create a *Point Helper*.
   ```
   Create Tab > Helpers > Standard > Point
   ```
2. Align the *Point Helper* to the *COG Bone* in position only.
   ```
   [Select Point Helper] > Main Toolbar > Align
   ```
3. Color the *COG* control yellow.
   ```
   [Select Point Helper] > Name and Color > Color Swatch
   ```
4. Parent the controller under the "CTRL" group.
5. Parent the *Point Helper* under the "RIG" group.
6. Freeze *Transforms* of the controller.
   ```
   [Select controller] > Alt + Right-Click > Transform >
   Freeze Transform > Pop-Up Menu > Yes
   ```
7. Use the *Link Constraint* from the *COG Bone* to the *Point Helper*.
   ```
   [Select COG Bone] > Main Toolbar > Animation >
   Transform Controllers > Link Constraint > [Select Point
   Helper]
   ```
8. Use a *Link Constraint* from the *Point Helper* to the controller.
   ```
   [Select Point Helper] > Main Toolbar > Animation >
   Transform Controllers > Link Constraint > [Select
   controller]
   ```

Figure 5.2

The completed *COG* setup is extremely simple.

5.3.2 Torso, Spine and Head

We're going to create a nifty custom *Forward Kinematics* setup for the upper section of the creature. This upper section includes what I'm calling the torso, spine and head – I know that this probably has a very specific name, but that's not important for us riggers.

Anyway, this fancy setup we're about to create allows use direct control over each *Bone* in both rotation and position. The fact the position can be manipulated is what makes this setup special as it allows us to use the editable positions to fake squash and stretch in our creature. Now this is not as good as using scale, but it does mean that it will be real-time engine ready. Additionally, we'll be adding additional transform controllers to each of the animatable controls – this is going to give us the opportunity to use an extra control that has direct influence over the rotation of all of the controls... Let's jump into it and this will make sense soon enough.

Select all of those controls that we have for the upper section of this creature (Figure 5.3), but don't select the controls for the exhausts, as we'll tackle those in the next section. Make sure that the pivot of each of the controls is aligned to its respective *Bone* in both position and orientation. From there, use the *Select and Link* tool to put them into a hierarchy, with the highest control being at the bottom of the hierarchy so that it is affected by its parents. Link up this chain of controls to the *COG* control we created earlier and then go through and rename them correctly.

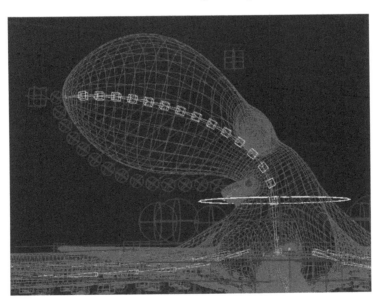

Figure 5.3

The upper section of Pheridan has many controls that can all be used to put this creature into various positions and poses.

Finish up the setup for these controls by coloring them a vibrant yellow and freezing transformations on all of them. We can now move onto creating *Point Helpers* which are aligned by position and rotation to each of the *Bones* on the skeleton chain. These need to be linked in a single hierarchy, linked back to the *COG Point Helper*, renamed correctly and their transforms frozen. I decided to color these *Point Helpers* in yellow, too, just so that they are easy to spot while we're rigging things.

Creating a Custom Forward Kinematic Setup for the Upper Section of Pheridan (Torso, Spine and Head)

1. Check that the control pivots are aligned by both position and rotation to their respective *Bones*.
   ```
   [Select Control] > Hierarchy Tab > Pivot > Affect Pivot
   Only
   ```

2. Use the *Select and Link* tool to add them into a single hierarchy that is attached to the *COG* control
   ```
   Main Toolbar > Select and Link
   ```

3. Rename the controls and color them yellow.

4. *Freeze Transformations* on the controls.
   ```
   [Select Controls] > Alt + Right-Click > Transform >
   Freeze Transform > Popup Menu > Yes
   ```

5. Create *Point Helpers* align in position and rotation to each of the *Bones* in the spine.
   ```
   Create Tab > Helpers > Standard > Point
   ```

6. Link all of these *Point Helpers* into one hierarchy connect back to the *COG Point Helper*.
   ```
   Main Toolbar > Select and Link
   ```

7. Rename, *Freeze Transformations*, and if you'd like to, you could color them yellow.
   ```
   [Select Controls] > Alt + Right-Click > Transform >
   Freeze Transform > Popup Menu > Yes
   ```

8. Constrain the *Bones* to their respective *Point Helpers* using *Position and Orientation Constraints*.
   ```
   [Select Bone] > Animation Menu > Constraints > Position
   Constraint > [Point Helper]
   [Select Bone] > Animation Menu > Constraints >
   Orientation Constraint > [Point Helper]
   ```

9. Use a *LookAt Constraint* to make each *Bone* aim at the next *Point Helper* while making the *Upnode* its own *Point Helper*.
   ```
   [Select Bone] > Animation Menu > Constraints > LookAt
   Constraint > [Point Helper]
   [Select Bone] > Motion Tab > Parameters > PRS
   Parameters > Rotation > LookAt Constraint > Select
   Upnode > Uncheck World > [Point Helper]
   ```

10. Use *Position and Orientation Constraints* to connect the *Point Helpers* to their controls.
    ```
    [Select Point Helper] > Animation Menu > Constraints >
    Position Constraint > [Control]
    [Select Point Helper] > Animation Menu > Constraints >
    Orientation Constraint > [Control]
    ```

We can now attach the *Bones* to each of the *Point Helpers* by using *Position Constraints* and *Orientation Constraints*. This allows those *Point Helpers* to control the position and rotation of the *Bones* which is great, and for the rotation, this all works out fine. However, you will notice that moving these the *Bones* comes along just fine, but they appear not to retain their connection to the next *Bone* in the chain. This is something we need to fix.

Add a *LookAt Constraint* to the first spine *Bone* and aim it toward the *Point Helper* above it. This may spin the *Bone* into an undesirable angle, but there's no need to worry – change the *Upnode* value from *World* to the *Point Helper* that sits at the base of the *Bone*. Now everything should work as expected and the incorrect flipping should be gone. Continue this procedure for all of the *Bones* in the spine hierarchy.

Now we can add *Position and Orientation Constraints* from each *Point Helper* to its control. This will complete the main spine rig setup, meaning that when the controls are manipulated, the creature will react correctly (Figure 5.4).

Technically, the custom FK spine setup is now complete and we could move on to another section of the creature's rig, or we could do one little enhancement that will

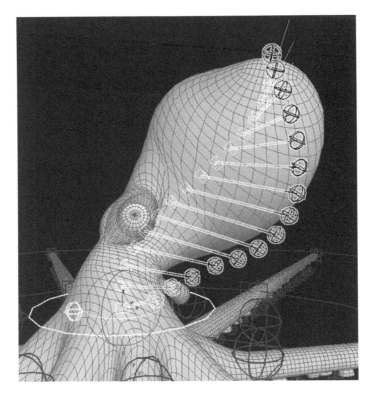

Figure 5.4

The spine rig for Pheridan is complete and manipulation of the controllers now affects the geometry.

make this spine setup even better. The next steps are completely optional, but for just a little more effort, we can have a more advanced custom FK spine setup, explore layered transform controllers and give things an even easier level of control – totally worth it.

The option is there for us to be able to use the controller at the front of the creature to additively control the multiple spine controllers at the rear of the creature. This allows for an easy-to-use single controller to manipulate all of the other controllers. Those other controllers can then become the extra controls if it is needed for certain poses. So, select that front controller, rename it, color it yellow, align its rotation pivot to that of the first spine *Bone*, then parent it to the *COG* control and *Freeze Transformations* on it. This will give us a clean controller to work with.

Next up is adding another transform controller to each of the spine controls. If this is new to you, it may get a little confusing, but at its most basic level, each object has a transform controller, let's say THE position. When moved, we get the output values of that position controller. For instance, moving the object from the center of the scene (*XYZ [0,0,0]*) by 5 units in *X* will give us a reading of *XYZ[5,0,0]*. If we then parent that to another object and move the parent object, that reading of *XYZ [5,0,0]* will stay the same as it reads its data from its parent instead of *world space*. We can actually set that same kind of system up, whereby we transform the object and get an output reading, then have another transform controller (which can be *wired* to another object) transform it. It's maybe easier just to do this and things will make more sense…

Select one of the spine controls and head to the *Motion* tab where in the *Assign Controller* section, we have the ability to expand the lists in there and see what transform controllers already exist. If we expand the *Rotation* section, there is an *Available* option, as shown in Figure 5.5. Highlight the *Available* option, then

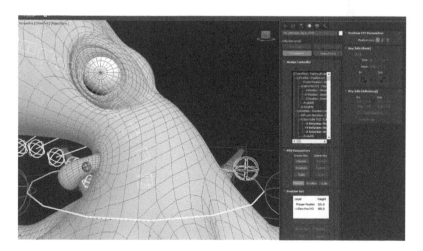

Figure 5.5

The *Motion* tab gives us easy access to the *Transform Controllers* of objects in our scenes.

click the *Assign Controller* button to open a new window with options for various transform controllers that we can assign.

Select the *Eular XYZ* option and click *OK* to add it to the selected control. All that's left to do is *wire* the *Zero Eular XYZ* rotations of the control at the front of the creature to the *Eular XYZ* rotations of the controls at the rear of the creature in a one-way connection.

Layering Transform Controllers to Create Additional Manipulation Options for the Spine Rig

1. Rename the front control and color it yellow.
2. Align its rotation pivot to the first spine *Bone*.
   ```
   [Select Object] > Hierarchy Tab > Pivot > Affect Pivot
   Only
   ```
3. Parent it to the *COG* control.
   ```
   [Select Object] > Main Toolbar > Select and Link
   ```
4. *Freeze Transformations* on the control.
   ```
   [Select Object] > Alt + Right-Click > Transform >
   Freeze Transform
   ```
5. On a spine control, assign an *Eular XYZ* controller to the *Available* option.
   ```
   [Select Object] > Motion Tab > Parameters > Assign
   Controller > Transform > Rotation > Available > Assign
   Controller > Eular XYZ > OK
   ```
6. Make a one-way *Wire Parameters* connection from the *Zero Eular XYZ* rotations of the control at the front of the creature to the *Eular XYZ* rotations of the control at the rear.
   ```
   [Select Object] > Right-Click > Wire Parameters...
   ```
7. Repeat steps 1 to 6 for all controllers in the spine's hierarchy.

Repeat this same procedure for each rotation axis, and that rear control can then be rotated both by itself and from the front controller in all axes. Duplicate this same setup for all of the controllers at the rear of the spine and we can really wrap up this part of the rig for Pheridan.

5.3.3 Exhausts

The exhausts of Pheridan are a much simpler setup that doesn't require anything too specific or complicated. The controllers for this section need to have their pivots aligned to the first exhaust *Bones* in rotation only. From there they can be parented to the second spine control, renamed, colored and their transforms frozen (Figure 5.6).

We can then add a *Position Constraint* from the first exhaust *Bone* to the control. I'm then wiring parameters from the rotation of the control to the first and second *Bones* of the exhaust. Incredibly, that finishes up the setup for both of these exhaust areas.

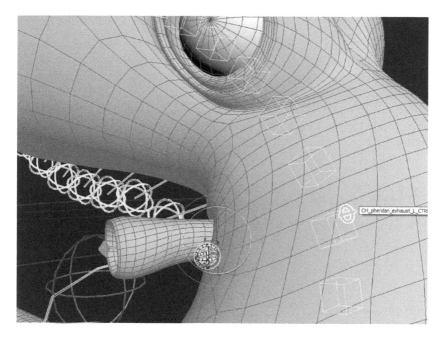

Figure 5.6

The exhausts are a quick and simple setup which allows us to easily complete the upper section of the Pheridan rig.

Pheridan's Exhaust Rig

1. Align the pivots of the control to the first exhaust *Bone* in rotation only.
   ```
   [Select Object] > Hierarchy Tab > Pivot > Affect Pivot
   Only
   ```
2. Parent them into the spine hierarchy. I'm using the second spine control.
   ```
   [Select Object] > Main Toolbar > Select and Link
   ```
3. Rename the control and color it yellow.
4. *Freeze Transform* on the control to reset it.
   ```
   [Select Object] > Alt + Right-Click > Transform > Freeze
   Transform
   ```
5. Create a *Position Constraint* from the first exhaust *Bone* to the control.
   ```
   [Select Object] > Animation Menu > Constraints >
   Position Constraint
   ```
6. Wire the rotations of both *Bones* to the rotations of the control in a one-way connection where the control affects the *Bones*.
   ```
   [Select Object] > Right-Click > Wire Parameters...
   ```

5.3.4 The Beak

The sections of the beak control need to be linked to the outer beak control and that outer beak control linked to the *COG* control so that they move along with the main hierarchy of controls. Align the pivots of the beak control sections to their respective *Bones* in both position and orientation. Then, as we usually do, rename the controllers and color them – I'm using yellow for the outer control and blue for the sections. Finish up the controls by freezing transforms (Figure 5.7).

Figure 5.7

The beak rig is another quick and easy section of the Pheridan creature.

5. Pheridan: Animation Rig

Pheridan's Beak Rig

1. Parent the controls into the main hierarchy: the two sections to the outer control and the outer control to the *COG*.
   ```
   [Select Object] > Main Toolbar > Select and Link
   ```
2. Align the pivots of the section controls to their respective beak *Bones* in both position and rotation.
   ```
   [Select Object] > Hierarchy Tab > Pivot > Affect Pivot
   Only
   ```
3. Rename the controls and color the controls in yellow and blue.
4. *Freeze Transform* on the controls to reset them.
   ```
   [Select Object] > Alt + Right-Click > Transform > Freeze
   Transform
   ```
5. Create a *Position Constraint* from each beak *Bone* to its respective control.
   ```
   [Select Object] > Animation Menu > Constraints >
   Position Constraint
   ```
6. Create an *Orientation Constraint* from each beak *Bone* to its respective control.
   ```
   [Select Object] > Animation Menu > Constraints >
   Orientation Constraint
   ```

All that's left to do is to add a *Position and Orientation Constraint* to the *Bones* so that they follow along with the beak section controls. We can then move onto the most challenging section of this creature, the limbs.

5.3.5 Tentacles (The Limbs)

As with everything in the world of 3D rigging, there are multiple ways to create a rig, multiple ways to build specific setups and multiple ways in which to craft sections and elements. It's always important to keep in mind that there is no right or correct way to do things. Sure, if a rig completely misses its purpose, then we could look at this as a failure, but I've yet to see any kind of rig that doesn't do at least one or two of the things it is meant to. With that said, we obviously always aim to create great rigs, but with so many options and possibilities it is sometimes difficult to find the right mix of what to create and provide. Of course we have our planning and preparation to help us out, along with the knowledge of what we need the creature rig to actually do, so we have at least some kind of starting point.

A squid or octopus rig like what we have with Pheridan can be as simple or as complex as it needs to be. Again, this all comes down to what we need this creature to actually do. For the purposes of this book and the explanations in this "Tentacles" section, I'm going to attempt to combine a few techniques together so

---

that we have a rig that demonstrates a number of viable possibilities for use when we rig tentacles or creatures like Pheridan.

What this means is that not all limbs of the Pheridan rig will be the same, but these different setups should form good demonstrations of the kinds of things that can be possible for this kind of rig. I'll be using a compass-style naming convention as we work around the limbs of the creature. The first limb, the one at the front of Pheridan, will be "North" or "N" in the case of our naming. The rearmost tentacle is "South," or "S." And I'm sure that you can work out the rest as we go.

5.3.5.1 North Limb

We'll start things out with an easy setup – a custom forward kinematic setup. Crazy, I know... Or maybe it's more boring than anything else, but as we've already set one of these up for the spine of this creature, it shouldn't take us too much time to recreate it for the limb. Also, as this is a pretty versatile setup, it should work very nicely for this tentacle.

First up is to create *Point Helpers* located at each of the *Bones* on the North limb. These should be linked together in one hierarchy and parented back into the *COG Point Helper*. *Freeze Transformations* on these, rename accordingly and color however you desire. Fix up the controls to have the same pivot positions and rotations, rename, make into one hierarchy, link to the COC control, color and *Freeze Transforms*.

Constraints next! Each *Bone* needs a *Position and Orientation Constraint* applied to its respective *Point Helper*. Then there needs to be a *LookAt Constraint* added so that it looks at the *Point Helper* in front of it and has its *Upnode* assigned as the *Point Helper* behind it. All that's left from there is to *Position and Orientation Constrain* the *Point Helpers* to their own controls.

That finishes the North limb setup (Figure 5.8). You will notice that I'm not including any step-by-step guide here, as this really is exactly the same as the custom FK in the spine, which we covered earlier. So if you do get stuck, check back through this chapter and refresh your memory on things before moving on.

5.3.5.2 East Limb

I actually debated putting a straight *Inverse Kinematic* chain into the setup for any of these limbs, but it is a valid option for some kinds of control schemes, even if it is deeply flawed. So, don't expect great things out of a straightforward *IK* rig on these kinds of tentacle-style limbs (Figure 5.9), but let's set one up anyway so that you have the benefit of seeing how this might or might not be an option for you.

This is also a good point to introduce or reintroduce you to creating *Custom Attributes* in 3ds Max. These *Custom Attributes* will allow us to gain access to more complex controls that may be hidden away from a general user of 3ds Max.

Figure 5.8

The completed North limb for Pheridan is exactly the same kind of setup that we created for the spine system.

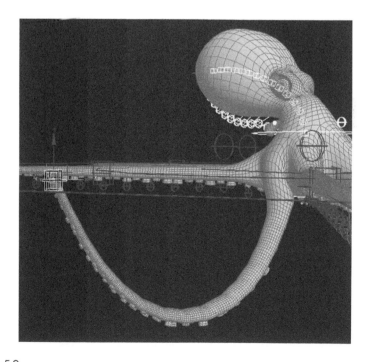

Figure 5.9

A straightforward *Inverse Kinematic* setup can be used for tentacle-style limbs, but keep in mind that the control available for this is limited and deeply flawed.

Creating Custom Attributes

1. On any object in 3ds Max, select it and head over to the *Parameter Editor*.
   ```
   [Select Object] > Animation Menu > Parameter Editor...
   (Alt + 1)
   ```
2. Edit and change all of the options available in the newly created *Parameter Editor* window and click the *Add* button to add a custom attribute to the selected object.
   ```
   [Select Object] > Parameter Editor > [Edit/Change
   Properties] > Add
   ```

To set up this rig along with a practical and usable custom attribute, create a *HI Solver* which runs from the first *Bone* to the end *Bone* of the East limb. This will create an *IK Solver* chain which is selectable in the viewports. Rename this and parent it to the controller at the end of the limb. Parent the controller up to the *COG* control, rename, *Freeze Transforms* and color.

With the control still selected, add an *Attribute Holder* to it, then add a custom attribute named "Twist." Make sure that this custom attribute is a *Float* and that the *Range* has the following parameters:

- From: –10.0
- To: 10.0
- Default: 0.0

Creating the East Limb

1. Create an *HI Solver* from the first *Bone* to the end.
   ```
   [Select Bone] > Animation Menu > IK Solvers > HI Solver
   > [Select End Bone]
   ```
2. Parent this to the control. Parent the control to the *COG* control and rename it, *Freeze Transformations* and color.
3. Add an *Attribute Holder* to the control.
   ```
   [Select Control] > Modify Tab > Modifier List >
   Attribute Holder
   ```
4. Add a custom attribute named "Twist" that operates from *–10.0 to 10.0* with a *0.0 Default* value.
   ```
   [Select Control] > Animation Menu > Parameter Editor...
   (Alt + 1)
   ```
5. Wire the *Twist* attribute from the control to the *Swivel Angle* of the *IK Solver*.
   ```
   [Select Object] > Right-Click > Wire Parameters... >
   Modified Object > Attribute Holder > Custom_Attributes >
   Twist > [Select IK] > Transform > Swivel Angle
   ```

Click the *Add* button to add this custom attribute to the *Attribute Holder. Wire* our created *Twist* attribute into the *IK solvers' Swivel Angle* and this will give us direct control over the twisting of the *IK* setup (Figure 5.10).

Once you have this setup complete, take a few minutes to test the kind of control that we are able to have in this kind of setup. You should note that it is fast and easy to pose, but the deformations are not great and getting the limb into all positions that we may desire is just not possible.

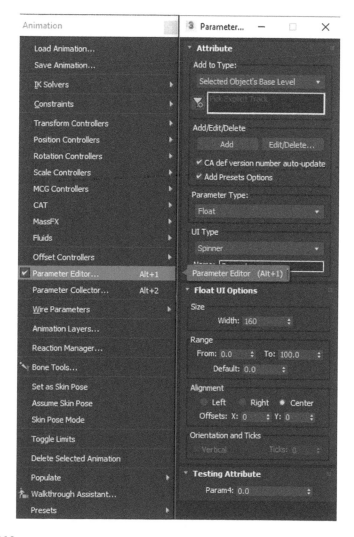

Figure 5.10

Using the *Parameter Editor* allows us to add custom attributes to any object that we have in our scene.

5.3.5.3 West Limb

We've created a custom *FK* limb and a basic *IK* limb, so we should honor the trio of standard kinematics by creating a standard *Spline IK* limb. In fact, using a *Spline IK* system is possibly one of the better setups for tentacle rigging. We're just going to create a basic system this time, but we'll use this as a base for more complex systems as we work through the rest of the limbs.

Run a *Line* from the first *Bone* to the end, making sure that there is a vertex for each *Bone* as you work down the chain. This will give us a *Line* that traces the *Bone* chain as accurately as possible. Rename, color and parent up to the *COG* locator. Then add a *Normalize Spline* modifier and change the *Max Knots* attribute to 4. This will change the look of the *Line* slightly, but it's nothing to worry about.

Creating The West Limb

1. Create a *Line* from the first *Bone* to the end, making sure to place a vertex at each *Bone* in the chain.
   ```
   [Create Tab] > Shapes > Splines > Line
   ```
2. Rename, color in red and parent up to the *COG* locator.
3. Use the *Normalize Spline modifier* to change the *Max Knots* to 4.
   ```
   [Select Object] > Modify Tab > Modifier List >
   Normalize Spline > Max Knots > [4]
   ```
4. Create a *Spline IK* system which runs from the first to the last *Bone* and uses the *Line* that we just created.
   ```
   [Select First Bone] > Animation Menu > IK Solvers >
   SplineIK Solver > [Select End Bone] > [Select Line]
   ```

Next up we can add a *Spline IK* system to the *Bones* and make sure that the created *Point Helpers* have the *Link All in Hierarchy* option enabled. Color and rename these as we always do, then parent everything into the hierarchy just like we keep doing like in Figure 5.11.

Now when we manipulate the *Point Helpers*, this limb behaves in a fantastically believable way for a tentacle. All that is left to do is to create controls and link things up correctly. I'm going to leave the *Point Helpers* out and exposed for this limb. This wouldn't be suitable for a production-ready rig, but in order to demonstrate the *Spline IK* setup a little more, I think that this is helpful.

5.3.5.4 South Limb

The setup for the South limb takes its foundations from the Western limb by using the exact same *Spline IK* setup. Once this setup has been duplicated, it is a simple case of going into the *Modify Tab* and experimenting with different *Modifiers*. No, really! Experimentation is in my opinion the best way to learn about all of the cool features, tools and secrets that 3ds Max holds. There are a number of great *Modifiers* built into this software and they are often underused, forgotten about or

Figure 5.11

The West limb is a simple setup, but it works incredibly well for the needs of tentacles.

just completely unknown to the user. The time spent testing out and researching as many of these *Modifiers* as possible is time well spent, as these new tips and tricks you learn from your experimentation can be of great use in other aspects of your rigging or in your general use of 3D and this software application.

I'm particularly fond of the *Bend* modifier for these kind of tentacle rigs, and I'm sure that you can tell exactly what this does without me having to explain it. Another great *Modifier* is the *Twist* modifier, but you may notice that this doesn't really work in the way that you might expect it to. Thing is, it does actually work incredibly well, but on this kind of *Spline IK* system, the twisting of things doesn't work correctly. Actually, you may have noticed that upon more extreme positioning and posing of the *Spline IK* setups that things can break. This is due to the limitations in twisting of the *Spline IK Solver* that is built into 3ds Max. I won't go into the details of these problems, but they are there, they have been since the solver's introduction and they are annoying. Luckily, there are solutions and ways to combat these shortcomings, but it is not particularly straightforward, quick or exactly simple to set up…

5.3.5.5 North East Limb

In order to get the *Spline IK* solver to work correctly, we have to go ahead and create our own custom *Spline IK* system (Figure 5.12). It's not incredibly difficult to create, but it is frustrating that this is still such a flawed part of the 3ds Max software. But, we'll make this work!

Figure 5.12

The custom *Spline IK* system behaves much more competently than the flawed built-in *Solver* that 3ds Max ships with.

Creating the North East Limb

1. Create a *Line* from the top to the bottom *Bones* and place a vertex at each *Bone* in the chain.
2. Create a *Point Helper* and *Path Constrain* it to the *Line*.
   ```
   [Select Point Helper] > Animation Menu > Constraints >
   Path Constraint > [Select Line]
   ```
3. Remove the animation that was automatically applied to the % *Along Path* attribute.
4. Turn on the *Follow* attribute.
   ```
   [Select Point Helper] > Motion Tab > Parameters > Path
   Parameters > Follow
   ```
5. Duplicate the *Point Helper* for each *Bone* in the limb's chain and position them at the start of each *Bone*.
6. Add a *Normalize Spline modifier* to the *Line* and change the *Max Knots* to 4.
7. Add a *Spline IK Control modifier* to the *Line* and change the *Link Types* to *No Linking*.
8. Create more *Point Helpers* aligned to the *Point Helpers* on the *Line* by *Position and Orientation*. Then move them away from that line in a single axis.
9. *Position Constrain* each *Bone* to its own *Point Helper* on the *Line* (you may need to turn on *Keep Initial Offset*).
10. Use a *LookAt Constraint* one each *Bone* pointing towards the next *Point Helper* and set the *Upnode* to be its respective *Point Helper* that now sits away from the line (you may need to turn on *Keep Initial Offset*).

---

5. Pheridan: Animation Rig

Oh, I should point out that what we are going to create for this custom system is nothing more than the spine rig that was created in the Belraus rig in the book *Digital Creature Rigging: The Art and Science of CG Creature Setup in 3ds Max*. If you have access to that book, and you really should (yes, self-promotion right now), then you can just check out that section and recreate it for this North East limb rig.

We have now created a custom *Spline IK* system which works great as we move the controllers around. If you notice any flipping, simply head back into the *LookAt Constraint* options and start adjusting the various axis parameters, which will fix everything up just great. The only thing that is left to do is that if we want to rotate this setup, we are sadly out of luck, but we will set that up on the next limb!

5.3.5.6 North West Limb

Pheridan's North West limb rig has the same rig as the North East limb – a custom *Spline IK* system. So that's the first thing that we need to create, and it's a simple case of following the exact same steps to recreate it. From there on out, we need to create another set of *Point Helpers* which will be placed at the already existing *Spline IK Control Point Helpers* from the custom setup. These new *Point Helpers* need to be parented together into one hierarchy so that they can work just like an *FK Bone* chain. Once they are behaving correctly, use the *Select and Link* tool to connect the *Point Helpers* which control the *Spline IK* system up to these new *FK Point Helpers*. Now when we rotate the *FK Point Helpers*, the *IK* system comes along for free and we can use that as additional control over the *FK* setup!

5.3.5.7 South East and South West Limbs

We have looked into six different options for the kinds of setups we can create for tentacles, and this is all within this chapter alone! As we already have so many choices available to us, I'm leaving the last two limbs entirely up to you. So, whichever setup you found best for your needs, go and revisit that setup and attach it to these two remaining tentacles.

In fact, if you're feeling adventurous, it is possible to combine all of these various setups into one tentacle. It is time consuming and possibly overkill, but the option is entirely up to you!

5.3.6 Layout

The final piece of the puzzle is to make sure that Pheridan can be moved into starting position anywhere in a scene. This becomes possible once we have created the very simple setup for the layout control. There is nothing interesting or taxing here, it is just a simple case of putting everything under one hierarchy with this layout control being the top in the control category (Figure 5.13).

Figure 5.13

The completed Pheridan rig.

5.4 Summary

This concludes the animation rig for the Pheridan creature. We took the *Bones* directly from the *Base Rig* and built a control system around it that allows us to manipulate this creature in a number of different ways. The tentacles – these limbs in particular allowed us to explore many different ways of setting up the rig. Sure, we could have created just one rig and duplicated that to each of the limbs, but creating the same rig eight times is never going to be fun. Instead, we have six different ways of rigging a tentacle, we've looked into the pros and cons of these setups and we've even explored the fact that all of these setups can be combined together to get the best options from all of these different techniques.

One thing that we didn't do in this chapter is create specific controllers for the various setups that we have made. This was a deliberate choice, as we've already discussed, and gives you the opportunity to experiment with different controls and controllers which you find most suitable for these kinds of setups.

Oh, and there is another thing... We set up six different tentacle rigs that can be used for manual keyframe animation and creature posing. We even left two tentacles open for exploration and experimentation in the combination of these methods, but we didn't discuss how we can get this squid to actually swim. You see, the controls that we have in place already are a perfectly viable option to animate the creature swimming in the ocean, or doing pretty much anything else, for that matter. However, there is a way to automatically give animation to these tentacles to make it look like the creature is swimming – completely automated with no time-consuming hand-keyed animations. So, how do we do that? Well, let's take a look at that kind of solution in the next chapter!

6

Pheridan

Deformation Rig

The giant squid is the perfect embodiment of a sea monster: it is huge, it has tentacles, it has big eyes, and it is absolutely frightening-looking. But, most important, it is real. Unlike the Loch Ness monster, we know it's out there.

David Grann

With the animation rig complete, we have a workable setup that can be used for key framed animation or creature posing. The multiple solutions we used for each of the tentacles can cause us some troubles if we're not careful, so if you wish, you may prefer to pick your favorite setup and duplicate that for each limb. But, as we move forward through this text, we'll be using the finished creature rig that includes the different setups for each limb, as the deformations on the skin of this creature need to look good no matter what kind of system we throw at it.

We're going to start things off by taking a look at the face of Pheridan to see if there is anything we can add from a real rigging point of view to enhance this rig further. After that, we'll revisit the creature's skinning information to check if there is any chance that we can make any improvements. Finally, we will discuss more advanced techniques, methods and deformers that we could possibly add to our setup to make this rig behave and deform as believably as possible.

But first …

6.1 Shot-Specific Rig: Automated Swimming Deformations

Although we finished the animation rig in the previous chapter, we created all of our controllers with the understanding that they would all be used for hand-keyed animation. This is perfectly fine, but we have the opportunity to add some pretty great automated controls to simulate our creature swimming in the ocean. In fact, the technique that we're going to use here can easily be applied to our manual animation rig as an additional control, and that is certainly my preferred way of doing things. However, to keep things more manageable and understandable for this book, let's create automated swimming deformations on their own shot-specific rig for now. You can of course replicate this method in your own rigs with or without additional manual animation controls. Anyway, let's get on with this – I'm working from the following file to start this shot-specific rig:

- 03_CH_Pheridan_SWIMSTART-RIG.max

We start this out with a pretty blank canvas (Figure 6.1). The spine section, exhausts and layout areas have been rigged to the specifications we set out during the creation of the animation rig, but the limbs are just *Bones* and nothing else. No rigging in there at all, so we should change that.

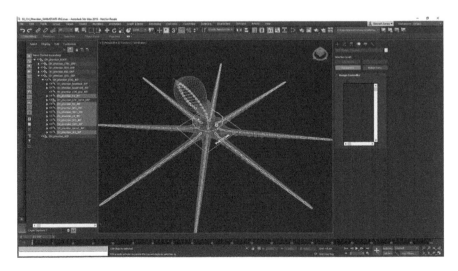

Figure 6.1

We start this section out with a blank canvas for the limbs. They're nothing more than the skinned *Bones* from the base rig at this point.

6. Pheridan: Deformation Rig

The first thing we need is a trusty *Point Helper* which needs to be positioned at the start of the *Bone* chain on one of the limbs. Next, we need to create a *Line* which has a vertex placed at the start of each *Bone* all the way to the end, this needs to be parented to the *Point Helper* and that *Point Helper* can be parented up to the *COG* locator so that everything is placed in one hierarchy.

As we have done many times before, we need to add a *Normalize Spline modifier* to the *Line*, making sure to set the *Max Knots* attribute to 6. Create a standard *Spline IK* system from the first to the last *Bone* and make sure that the created *Point Helper* controls are not linked into any hierarchy (Figure 6.2).

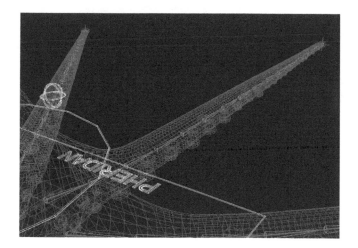

Figure 6.2

The creation of the *Spline IK* system for this setup is exactly the same as some of the setups that we created during the animation rig stage.

Link the created *IK* manipulator as well as the *Point Helpers* to the first *Point Helper* we created at the start of the *Bone* chain. This concludes the creation of the kinematics for the limb and gives us one very clean hierarchy to work with. It's now time to add the modifier that will allow us to give the impression that Pheridan is swimming.

Select the *Line* and add a *Wave* modifier to it. Find the *Center* option in the *Modify Tab* for this modifier and select it. This allows us to control where the center of this modifier evaluates from. We need to make sure that this is aligned in position to the first *Point Helper* sitting at the start of the limb. With the *Center* in the correct place, set the *Wave Length* attribute to *0.1 m...* And nothing happens!

Don't worry just yet; we're actually just about finished with this setup, and if you'd like some kind of visual feedback, you could change the *Amplitude 2* attribute and you will see that the limb is affected (Figure 6.3). What we've just done by editing that attribute is to start to control the *Wave* modifier, and we could technically use this to simulate the swimming motion, but we want to create

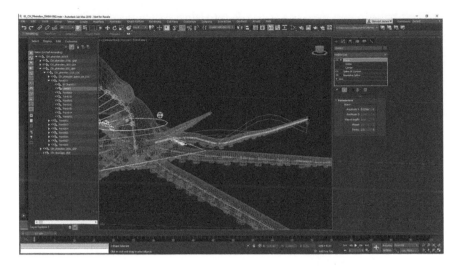

Figure 6.3

Changing the *Amplitude 2* attribute on the *Wave* modifier gives you a visual cue that the setup has been applied correctly.

something a little more sophisticated for the person who will animate this rig (even if it is us).

So, reset the *Amplitude 2* modifier if you haven't already and select the *COG* control. Add an *Attribute Holder* to this so that we clean up that *Modifier* tab area. We can then add our own custom attributes so that we have direct access to the attributes of that *Wave* modifier from a more logical place. I'm adding the following three custom attributes with specific settings which will work for this limb rig:

- Wave
  - Parameter Type: Float
  - UI Type: Slider
  - From: 0.0
  - To: 100.0
  - Default: 0.0
- Height
  - Parameter Type: Float
  - UI Type: Slider
  - From: 0.0
  - To: 1.0
  - Default: 0.0
- Motion
  - Parameter Type: Float
  - UI Type: Spinner

6. Pheridan: Deformation Rig

- From: –100.0
- To: 100.0
- Default: 0.0

With these custom attributes added to the *COG* control we can wire these in a one-way connection to the parameters found on the *Wave modifier*:

- Wave > Amplitude 2
- Height > Wave Length
- Motion > Phase

Adding a Wave Modifier to Simulate a Swimming Motion

1. Create a *Point Helper* and align its position to the start of the *Bone* chain.
2. Create a *Line* from the start to the end of the *Bone* chain and with a vertex placed at the start of each *Bone*.
3. Parent the *Line* to the *Point Helper*.
4. Create a *Spline IK* system which runs from the first to the last *Bone* and uses the *Line* for control.
5. Parent the newly created *Point Helpers* and the *IK chain* to the *Point Helper* at the start of the limb.
6. Add a *Normalize Spine* modifier to the *Line* and change the *Max Knots* to 6.
   ```
   [Select Line] > Modify Tab > Modifiers List > Normalize
   Spline > Max Knots > (6)
   ```
7. Add a *Wave* deformer to the *Line*.
   ```
   [Select Line] > Modify Tab > Modifiers List > Wave
   ```
8. Change the *Center* of the modifier so that it is positioned at the first *Point Helper*.
   ```
   [Select Line] > Modify Tab > Wave > Center
   ```

This really concludes the automation of a swimming motion for the tentacles. This setup needs to be duplicated for each limb for the creature and they all need to be wired correctly. Once complete, this kind of setup can really enhance the believability of our rig, but there's one more additional thing that we could add which would really bring it to the next level.

6.1.1 Adding Even More Automation

Just having the *Wave* modifier applied to each of the limbs has improved the usage of our rig tenfold. However, there is one more really simple thing which we can do that will make this swimming rig even better – even when the creature isn't swimming.

What I'm talking about is giving the limbs some *automatic overlapping action*. For those of you familiar with Disney's Twelve Principles of Animation, you will already know what I'm talking about. For the rest of us, automatic overlapping action refers to the movement of things after the initial action (movement) has taken place. Think of things like a coat or a character with long ears or a tail – after the character has finished its movement, there are other areas, like the ears, which may lag or drag behind before coming to a stop later. This is exactly the kind of behavior that we can add to Pheridan's tentacles without too much effort.

Adding Automatic Overlapping Action to the Tentacles

1. Select the *Line* and add a *Flex* modifier to it.
   ```
   [Select Line] > Modify Tab > Modifiers List > Flex
   ```
2. Move the *Center* of the *Flex* modifier to the *Point Helper* positioned at the start of the *Bone* chain for the limb.
   ```
   [Select Line] > Modify Tab > Flex > Center
   ```

There's really nothing difficult here. Simple grab hold of the *Line* that creates part of the *Spline IK* system for a tentacle and then add a *Flex* modifier to it. This *Flex* modifier works automatically and instantly. If you were to animate the *COG* right now, you would even see its effect on the limb that has it attached. To increase the effectiveness of this modifier and also the kind of reaction it has, move its *Center* to the position of the *Point Helper* at the start of the *Bone* chain for the tentacle. From there, jump back into the modifier's attributes and make sure the following is set correctly (Figure 6.4):

- Flex: 1.0
- Strength: 0.5
- Sway: 7.0

This should give you some really great looking automatic overlapping action for a tentacle and this modifier can be quickly copied and pasted to the other limb setups for Pheridan. To make it easier to access the attributes of this modifier, we can easily add a custom attribute to the *COG* control which should be wired to the *Sway* attribute on the *Flex* modifier as shown in Figure 6.4.

6.1.2 Finishing Up the Shot-Specific Rig

We're pretty much done with this shot-specific rig for Pheridan and all that is needed is a little clean-up to make this ready to go into animation. This would usually require us to lock down all of the controllers to make sure they have only the correct controls we want animators to use; it would also mean locking away any rig-specific nodes as well as hiding them from the view of others who will use our rig. However, for the purposes of this book I'll not be doing any of those

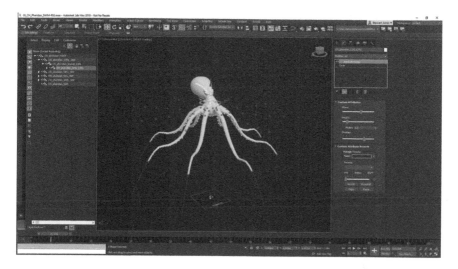

Figure 6.4

The effect and correct settings for the attributes on the *Flex* modifier as applied to the tentacles of Pheridan. A custom attribute can be added to the *COG* control to allow easy access to change the effects of this modifier.

things, which means that everything is easily accessible and completely visible in the viewports. I hope that this will make dissecting my rig a little easier and will hopefully speed up the learning process if you're trying to get access to any of the nodes, attributes or modifiers I've added on my journey with Pheridan's shot-specific rig so far. You can grab hold of this automated swimming and overlapping action rig from this file:

- 04_CH_Pheridan_SWIM-RIG.max

6.2 Pheridan's Face Rig

Back to the rig that we created earlier – the one with the various kinds of setups on each of the tentacles – we can start thinking about Pheridan's face rig. Oh, and we're working off the following file from here on out:

- 05_CH_Pheridan_RIG.max

Pheridan's face, or lack thereof, is nothing more than two huge eyes. In fact, during the base rig, we already attached the *Skin* modifier, which gave us a first step into the deformation of this area. What happened during that stage was the need to keep the area around the eyes as rigid as possible or the deformations as the *Bones* moved and rotated just looked weird. What this means for us is that most of our job is already done for us. Woohoo!

Having said that, Pheridan right now has no emotion, can't look around and can't even blink… Although he could technically talk if it was possible, as the beak area works pretty great. Anyway, we won't solve all of its emotive problems right now, but we can make this creature blink at the very least. To do this we're going to use a technique that isn't always available in real-time engines, but is always available for prerendered technology. What I'm talking about is *Morphs* and the *Morpher* modifier.

I'm sure that you're already well aware of what these things are, but just to be safe, we'll be creating a system in which we can use one set of geometry to completely deform another by a way of *morphing* between the two. These two are the base, where the *Morpher* modifier is applied, and the target, where the geometric changes have been made. This may sound complicated if you're new to this, and honestly the mathematics and procedures behind it are very complex, but the actual practical application for us working in 3ds Max is relatively straightforward.

Okay, let's just create a blink system for Pheridan, which should be easy enough for those used to this procedure and logical enough for those new to it. We can use this same technique for many other face rig setups for this creature, but for what we need, just one of these is more than enough to demonstrate.

Start by duplicating the body geometry of Pheridan and delete the *Skin* modifier, as this is not needed. This duplicate geometry is going to become the target shape for our *Morpher* modifier and I suggest moving it away from the base geometry so that we can work on it easily like in Figure 6.5.

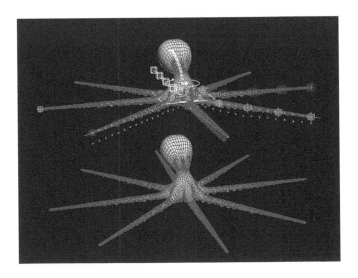

Figure 6.5

We need to duplicate the geometry so that we have both the base geometry and the target geometry which we can start to edit.

6. Pheridan: Deformation Rig

Select the base geometry once again and add a *Morpher* modifier to it. Be sure to move the *Morpher* modifier under the *Skin* modifier in the *Modifier Stack* or there will be problems with deformations and transformations going forward (check Figure 6.5 for the correct *Modifier Stack* layout). Add the duplicate geometry to the first *Channel* on the *Morpher* modifier and set it to *100.0* so that it is active. Also turn on the *Automatically reload targets* checkbox at the bottom of the *Channel List* so that any updates we make to the duplicate geometry will be displayed automatically on the main geometry (Figure 6.6).

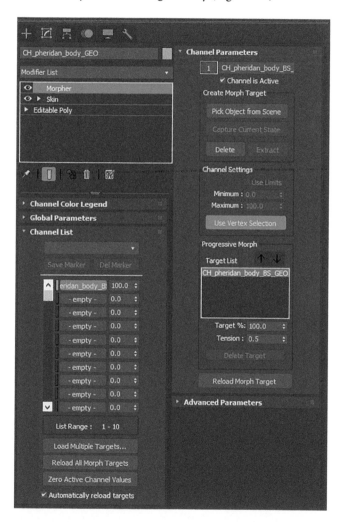

Figure 6.6

Adding the duplicate geometry to the *Morpher* modifier and setting it to *100.0* with *Automatically reload targets* checked lets us view any changes directly on the main geometry.

Setting up the Morpher Modifier

1. Duplicate the base geometry and move it somewhere else in the scene so it can be easily edited. Be sure to remove any modifiers that have been attached to it. If you have modifiers that have changed the geometry in any way, simply *Collapse All* in the stack.
2. Add a *Morpher* modifier to the main geometry and move it under the *Skin* modifier (if it is present).
   `[Select Geometry] > Modify Tab > Modifier List > Morpher`
3. Load the duplicate geometry as a target and set it to *100.0*.
4. Turn on *Automatically reload targets* by clicking the checkbox for this option at the bottom of the *Channel List* rollout.
5. Edit the duplicate geometry to see the results on the main model.

Okay, so now it's a case of editing the duplicate geometry, which is now the *Target* geometry. This can be easier said than done, as we have access to all of the tools we usually have when modeling in 3ds Max, but we have to be careful not to use any techniques or methods that change to vertex numbering – these are things like *Cut* and *Detach*, amongst others. Having said that, everything else is at our disposal, including many helpful modifiers. So, sit down, relax and get to model the blink position of the creature. We can use the main geometry to view how this will actually look when finished so there is no guess work to be done here (Figure 6.7).

To finish up, we can go ahead and add another custom attribute to the *COG* control and wire this up to control the blink target on the *Morpher* modifier.

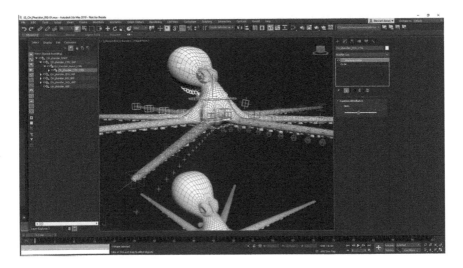

Figure 6.7

The finished *Morph* applied to the main geometry.

6. Pheridan: Deformation Rig

6.3 Perfecting the Deformations

There's not much left to do for the Pheridan rig, but if we spend just a little more time on the deformations that we have, this creature rig will look truly amazing. The first and most substantial thing that we can do is to revisit the skinning and skin weights that we already assigned during the base rig. Now that we have the completed rig in place and have no further needs to extend the complexity of it in any way, we now know exactly how the rig behaves, how it deforms and any areas which we can improve.

This may take some extra time, and making sure things look great can be a challenge, but the end visuals of this process are more than worth it. If there is nothing that specifically stands out as being "bad" right now, well, let me congratulate you for doing an incredible skinning job during the base rig stage, but I'm pretty confident that there are at least one or two things which could be improved with some tweaks here and there.

Once we are completely happy with the skinning, we could think about adding some additional deformers that may not be entirely necessary but could add a little something extra to our creatures. These extra deformers take place as modifiers, so they are quick and easy to set up and offer us the opportunity to wire custom attributes that we create to give us better control over them. Neat!

The deformers which can add a lot to our rigs are the *Stretch, Relax, Push* and *Noise* modifiers – the results of which are illustrated in Figure 6.8. The *Stretch* modifier allows us to easily attach squashing and stretching to our creatures and requires very little initial setup to look great.

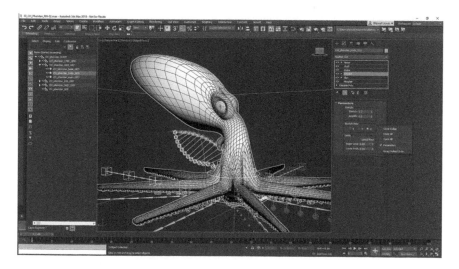

Figure 6.8

Applying additional modifiers such as this *Stretch* modifier can dramatically influence our geometry without breaking the underlying rig that we spent hours already creating.

The *Relax* modifier softens any geometry or object that it is attached to. This may not seem all that helpful at first, but as we are able to edit and change the parameters of the modifier as well as the ability to animate those attributes, we have something which can be used to enhance and minimally change skinning of our creatures. Very helpful if we need a quick fix for skinning problems or if we need to smooth and soften frames of animation or specific areas of the geometry.

Applying a *Push* modifier actually pushes and plumps out the geometry it is applied to. This is super useful for simulating the breathing of our creatures, or if we need the kind of ability to expand our creature's geometry in any way – it's a pretty cool thing for our squid creature to be able to do.

Finally, the *Noise* modifier is just fun! It adds a crazy noise-style deformation across the model, which looks crazy when applied at stronger/higher levels. When applied at lower levels, it can simulate cold or shivers, amongst other kinds of effects. It's definitely worth playing with to see what you can come up with.

Oh, and I have to mention that the previous deformers we have looked into will probably not work in a real-time engine due to the various limitations that they have, but for prerendered they are completely fine. Thing is, if your real-time engine supports morphs, there may be something that we could do...

6.3.1 Advanced Deformation Methodology

The problem with real-time engines is that they cannot accept many of the crazy and great deformers that are built into 3ds Max. Although it's understandable from a technical point of view, it is pretty frustrating when we're able to create a great effect inside of the 3ds Max application but it doesn't transfer into other software. There is a little trick that we can do, but before things get too exciting, things don't always work out, but it is something that we can try.

So, this technique requires us to use the *Morpher* modifier once again. This means that the real-time engine needs to be able to use morphs... At least one or two of them. If not, well, this just isn't going to work. Sorry. This technique is also fantastic if you need to add complicated and processor-intensive modifiers to our creatures but they perform slowly in the viewports when applied.

What I'm talking about is using a *Morpher* modifier on our base geometry, setting the *Target* to *100.0* and then applying all of the deformers to the target. I know that this doesn't seem all that revolutionary, but it is incredibly helpful for keeping modifier data to a minimum on our main creature and adding all of the crazy stuff to a single morph target. Try this out if you're having any trouble with modifier-heavy rigs slowing down your scenes. I think you'll be surprised at the increase in performance for such a simple change to your rigging technique.

6.3.2 World-Space Modifiers and Space Warps

All of the modifiers that we have used so far have referenced and used the *local space* of the objects that they are applied to. We have completely missed out on using any *World-Space Modifiers (WSM)* that used the *world space* for their reference. The difference between these kinds of modifiers is the simple case

Figure 6.9

Crazy and magical things can happen when we start using *World-Space Modifiers (WSM)*.

that one can only use the object it is applied to (local) and the other can use other objects in the scene (world). Generally, local-space modifiers are used more, but at odd times it can be great to use a WSM for some special kinds of deformations.

As a quick example, you can add a *Sphere* to the Pheridan scene and apply a *SurfDeform Binding (WSM)* modifier to the squid geometry. Initially it won't do anything at all, but change some settings and assign a surface, and crazy things happen (Figure 6.9).

Using a World-Space Modifier to Create a Whirlpool out of Your Creature's Geometry

1. Create a *Sphere* in Pheridan's scene.
   `Create Tab > Geometry > Standard Primitives > Sphere`
2. Apply a *SurfDeform Binding (WSM)* to Pheridan.
   `[Select Object] > Modify Tab > Modifiers List > SurfDeform Binding (WSM)`
3. Make sure that the following parameters are set on the modifier:
   - U Percent: 50.0
   - U Stretch: 1.0
   - V Percent: 50.0
   - V Stretch: 1.0
   - Rotation: 0.0
4. Click the *Pick Surface* button and choose the *Sphere* to see the effect that we have created.

Space Warps can also be applied to our creatures and we can enjoy all of the options that come along with them. There are many things that we can do with the fantastic extra options that they offer to us, and once again, there are so many of them, it is way out of the scope of this book to give much time to them. However, I'd like to show you a really neat trick that you may find useful for your creatures and other rigs you may be creating now and in the future.

Create a *Displace* object in the Pheridan scene and set its *Map* to *Spherical*. Change the *Length, Width* and *Height* attributes to *1.0 m* and you should be left with a *Spherical Displace* object in the scene. Update the *Strength* to *0.5 m* and the *Decay* to *1.0*, then position it away from the creature's geometry. We can now use the *Bind to Space Warp* tool to link the *Displace* object to the model.

Creating a Cool Effect using Space Warps

1. Add a *Displace* object to the Pheridan scene.
   ```
   Create Tab > Systems > Forces > Displace
   ```
2. Change the *Map* of the *Displace* object to *Spherical*.
3. Update the *Length, Width* and *Height* to *1.0* m each.
4. Edit the *Strength* parameter to *0.5* m and the *Decay* parameter to *1.0*.
5. Link the *Displace* object to the geometry with the *Bind to Space Warp* tool.
   ```
   Main Toolbar > Bind to Space Warp > Click and drag from
   Displace to object
   ```

Nothing will happen just yet, but if you select that *Displace* object and manipulate it so it passes through the geometry of Pheridan, you will see greatness happen (Figure 6.10). So cool!

Figure 6.10

We can create some truly fantastic effects by using *Space Warps* and modifiers.

Those are some pretty neat extras we've looked into for this section. I urge you to explore the other options that are available to you in these areas of the 3ds Max software. If you'd like to take a look at the finished *Displace* setup, please take a look at the following file:

- 04_CH_Pheridan_EXTRA_DEFORMATION.max

6.4 Summary

Outputs from this chapter reached far beyond the basic deformations that we're accustomed to, and what we ended up with was various tricks and techniques to really make our creatures shine. We created a custom shot-specific rig that automated swimming and gave flex to each of the limbs of the Pheridan creature. We then tackled the face of the creature and added a morph target to allow the creature to blink.

Once all of that was set up, we jumped into using additional deformers and modifiers to enhance our creature even more. Some effects were subtle, others extreme and some just for fun. We finished off this chapter by discussing deformation methodology at an advanced level by combing modifiers, *World-Space Modifiers (WSM)* and *Space Warps* – things usually found in effects tutorials rather than in a book for creature rigging. But hey, what's to stop us using everything that we can to create the best possible creature rigs? The answer is us, just ourselves. So let's use everything that we can!

We finish out this section with one more file:

- 06_CH_Pheridan_DEFORMATION.max

7

Xilteor

Base Rig

I believe in everything until it's disproved. So I believe in fairies, the myths, dragons. It all exists, even if it's in your mind. Who's to say that dreams and nightmares aren't as real as the here and now?

John Lennon

Moving above the waters and looking into the skies, we can now start working on the rig for the mythical dragon creature, Xilteor. This quadruped requires us to think about many different features that all need to work in a cohesive manner in order for us to deliver a successful creature rig.

As this is the starting point for our rig, we once again focus on the core foundations of this setup and make sure that the foundation that we are building is strong and sturdy to support the more complex upcoming rigging stages. We will create the core hierarchy for this dragon by using *Bones* and then work on some basic deformations using the *Skin* modifier. We'll actually be going through the same step-by-step process we did for the giant squid, Pheridan, but changing and adapting things to meet the needs and requirements of a dragon rig.

We will be working from the following file during this chapter:

- 01_CH_Xilteor_GEO.max

7.1 Core Hierarchical Structure

The first step is the same as always. We need to create the *ROOT* node, the node that will always sit at the very top of the hierarchical chain for this creature. I'll drop in an *ExposeTM Helper* object for this at the center of the scene, *XYZ [0,0,0]*. Please remember that this node won't work in some real-time engines, so a *Point Helper* is a better choice if that's where this creature rig is heading to.

This newly created *ROOT* node will be named *CH_xilteor_ROOT* if you're following along with the rigging of this creature. If you're working on your own creature rig, please name it accordingly.

Next we can add in all of the groups that will keep our rig clean and organized. The *CH_xilteor_GEO_GRP* is already in this scene from earlier, so we just need to add another four *Point Helpers* positioned in the center of the scene, *XYZ[0,0,0]*, and rename them correctly:

- CH_xilteor_CTRL_GRP
- CH_xilteor_RIG_GRP
- CH_xilteor_SKEL_GRP
- CH_xilteor_WIP

Link things up into one hierarchy and that's it!

7.2 Bone Creation and Placement

There's nothing new or special about how we're going to create the *Bones* for the Xilteor rig. It's the exact same tools and techniques that we've already been using, so it should be no surprise as to what comes next. In fact, the only real change is the placement of the *Bones* and the uses that we will be using them for. Let's take a look at that starting *Bone*, the *COG*.

7.2.1 Center of Gravity

Where does the movement originate from on this creature?

The question that always applies to the decision of where to place the *Center of Gravity* is the same here. Xilteor is an interesting creature in that his rear legs are huge and powerful, but his front legs are tiny and weak, even though this is where those huge wings span from. For me, this means that its *COG* would be placed at the hips when on the ground and walking, but would switch to the chest when in the air and flying. This leaves us with the dilemma of where to place the *COG* for its default position. Of course, we can us an *animatable pivot* to combat this problem, so it won't really cause any troubles for animation, but getting the initial placement as good as possible is always a good rule to have.

As this creature is featured on the cover image of this book in a flying position, I'm going to go ahead and place the *COG* at the chest. This might even be a little controversial, but hey, who's going to stop us experimenting right now? No one! (Figure 7.1).

Figure 7.1

Xilteor's *COG* is placed at its chest.

7.2.2 Hips, Head and Tail Fin

With the *COG* sitting in place at the chest, we can focus on another three single *Bone* chains that are quick and easy to create but also provide pivot locations for the large neck, spine and tail sections. The hip are just like the *COG* just placed at the hips – I know, no shock there!

The head should start from where we would like the neck to end and then exit towards the top of where the skull will be. This head *Bone* gives us a solid indicator of where we want the head to rotate from and where the neck *Bones* should stop affecting things.

At the rear of the creature, the tail fin should run from the end of the tail to the very end of the tail fin geometry. Again, another single *Bone* chain for this (Figure 7.2).

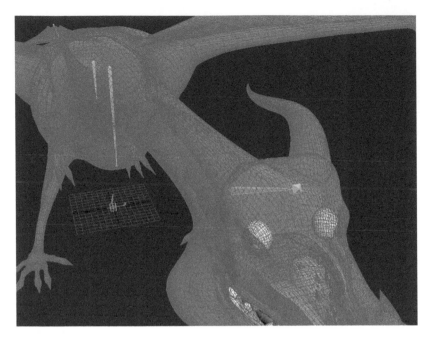

Figure 7.2

The head, *COG*, hips and tail fin *Bones* give specific pivot points for the neck, spine and tail to attach to.

7.2.3 Neck, Spine and Tail

The neck, spine and tail sections of this creature need to work together in order to increase its believability. This should be fluid and intuitive, maintaining connections to all areas of the creature. For instance, if the hips move, the tail needs to be affected in some way, and so on.

In order to create evenly spaced *Bones* throughout this setup, I'll be using the technique we covered in Chapter 4, "Pheridan: Base Rig," called "Creating, Editing, Rebuilding and Controlling Splines." So, be sure to check back to that section for reference as we work through this. Anyway, the first thing we need to do is to get a *Line* drawn from the end of the tail (using the tail fin *Bone* pivot) up to the hip, then to the *COG* and ending at the head *Bone* pivot. This *Line* is going to be pretty straight and linear or bending in all the wrong ways depending on the initial creation parameters you have set up. But, no matter which way it turned out, change the vertices to *Bezier handles* and edit them so they fit within the creature's geometry.

Once you're happy with the look of your *Line*, add a *Normalize Spline* modifier and set the *Max Knots* parameter to whatever works for you. In this Xilteor setup, I'm using a total of *25 Max Knots* (Figure 7.3). Now just add a *Spline IK Control* modifier and click the *Create Helpers* button to create *Point Helpers* that can be used as pivot points for our *Bones*.

7. Xilteor: Base Rig

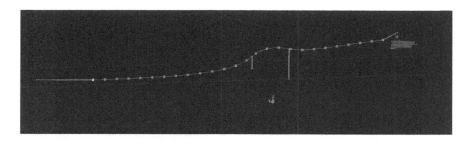

Figure 7.3

The completed *spline* setup for the neck, spine and tail section of Xilteor.

To finish up, create a *Bone* chain that runs from the pivot of the *COG* up to the head in order to create the neck, then a separate *Bone* chain from the *COG* to the hips and continuing down to the tail fin. This should leave you with two *Bone* chains that will create the neck, spine and tail. If you'd like to add some additional *Bones* into the tail fin, don't let me stop you, but it's completely optional.

7.2.4 Limbs

Xilteor's front legs are a two-*Bone* setup with its feet/paws/hands (whatever you want to call them) attached with a single *Bone*. Additional *Bones* are used for each digit and it's a relatively simple placement for everything (Figure 7.4).

At the rear legs I'm using a three-*Bone* chain for the main structure. The feet have a two-*Bone* chain, and additional *Bones* are placed for each digit and the extra claw on the reverse knee.

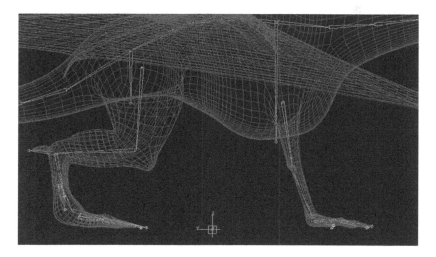

Figure 7.4

The limbs with *Bone* placement completed.

7.2.5 Wings

Each wing has a simple two-*Bone* chain for each of the "arm" structures. From there I've added additional two-*Bone* chains for each of the spines and for the extra claw. There's nothing special going on here, just a careful placement of these *Bones*, as shown in Figure 7.5.

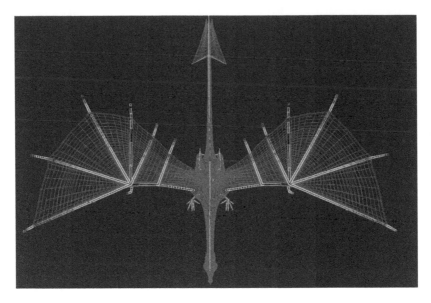

Figure 7.5

Xilteor's *Bone* setup for the wings has been kept as simple as possible.

7.3 Building the Skeletal Hierarchy

Remember to rename all of the *Bones* correctly before going any further. I know, boring, but it should be done to avoid any confusion later. With everything correctly named, we can go ahead and start using the *Select and Link* tool to start combing the *Bones* into one single hierarchy. Here's what I'm linking together:

- Head to the neck.
- Neck to the COG.
- Spine to the COG.
- Thumb to the hand.
- Index finger to the hand.
- Middle finger to the hand.
- Ring finger to the hand.
- Pinky finger to the hand.
- Hand to the arm.
- Arm to the COG.

- Toe inner to the foot.
- Toe middle to the foot.
- Toe outer to the foot.
- Foot to the leg.
- Ankle to the leg.
- Knee to the leg.
- Leg to the hip.
- Hip to the spine.
- Claw fingers to the wing.
- Elbow to the wing.
- Wing to the COG.

Heh! That's a lot more linking than what we had to do for Pheridan. Anyway, I've only been working on the *Bones* for one side of the creature right now, so I need to use the *Mirror* button on the *Bone Tools* rollout in order to flip them to the other side. With that done, it's another round of renaming and linking, then adding these *Bones* to the skeleton group in the main hierarchy. Then we can move on.

7.3.1 Local Rotation Axis

It's important to make sure the LRAs for Xilteor's *Bones* behave in a logical way, especially for the wings of this creature. We're doing nothing different this time, simply testing the local rotations of each of the *Bones*, and if they need to be changed, we turn on *Bone Edit Mode* on the *Bone Tools* rollout.

7.3.2 Location Information Data Node

Let's quickly add in the *Location Information Data Node* so that we can get ground-plane positional information if we need to. We can refer back to Chapter 4, "Pheridan: Base Rig," for the step-by-step procedures, but here's a quick-look version for your reference:

- Create a *Point Helper* positioned at *XYZ [0,0,0]*.
- Align its pivot point to the *COG*.
- Link it to the *COG*.
- Lock the *Move, Rotate and Scale*.
- Turn off the *Inherits* except for the *Move X,Y*.
- Create a *Bone* at the location of the *Point Helper*.
- Link the *Bone* to the *Point Helper*.

This completes everything for the skeleton of this creature (Figure 7.6); we can now move on to the skinning.

7.4 Base Skinning

For the eyes, tongue and teeth of Xilteor, we need to add a *Skin* modifier with only the head *Bone* attached to it. This is just temporary for this stage, of course,

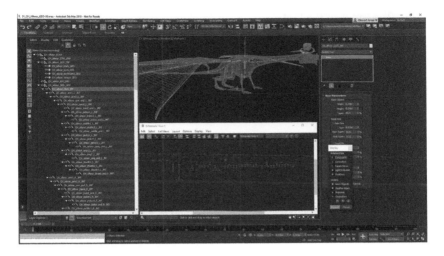

Figure 7.6

Xilteor's base hierarchy and completed *Bone* skeleton system.

but it will be helpful to have that geometry move along with the base rig and the skinning we're about to do on the body.

So, add another *Skin* modifier to the body geometry and add all of the *Bones* to the modifier, paying special attention not to add any of the "end" *Bones*. This will give the default *skin weighting* provided to each vertex by 3ds Max. We already know that this is not ideal, so we need to go in there and edit each *Bone's* skin weighting to *100%* for the correct vertices. We could spend hours looking into good weighting methods and techniques, but, as we've already covered this, we can just make sure to spend some care and attention getting this right like in Figure 7.7.

There's no need to skin both sides of this creature, as we can simply use the *Mirror* skinning tools provided for us by 3ds Max and the *Skin* modifier. In order to get this to work correctly, I had to increase the *Mirror Thresh* parameter to *0.187* m. After doing this, I was able to mirror the data from one side to the other by using the *Paste Green to Blue Verts* option.

Using the Mirror Skin Weights Tool

1. Select the object with the *Skin* modifier attached and enable the *Edit Envelopes* option.
   [Select Object] > Skin modifier > Edit Envelopes
2. Scroll down to the *Mirror Parameters* rollout and click the *Mirror Mode* button.
3. Skin modifier > Mirror Parameters > Mirror Mode
4. Edit and change the *Parameters* as needed before clicking on one of the mirror options to execute the mirroring.

7. Xilteor: Base Rig

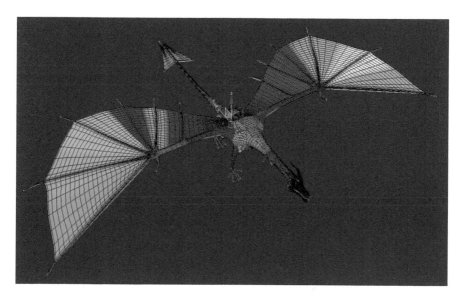

Figure 7.7

The finished blocking of the skin weights for Xilteor.

To finish up the blocking of the skin weighting, we need to head to the *Advanced Parameters* rollout on the *Skin* modifier. In there, we can click the *Remove Zero Weights* button and change the *Bone Affect Limit* to *4* or another number that works for your production and project.

7.4.1 Smooth Skinning

Taking this creature from a rough blocky skinning into smooth-skinned deformations is no easy task. Working out from the *COG* instantly starts us off on a challenge, as each of the spine *Bones* require us to take into consideration the wings on both sides of the body. These wings cause a number of troubles, as they are attached from the shoulders all the way down to the hips, so no matter what we do, everything has to work together seamlessly and throughout a lot of different movements.

The tail and head pose little challenge and the limbs are relatively straightforward too. More difficulties are thrown our way when we try to smooth the skinning on the wings of Xilteor. These are large areas which have to smoothly blend together as well as being able to flap and fold during flight or when the wings are closed when not needed. Add to this the various other forms of articulation this creature needs to be able to perform and I can tell you, this section took me many hours of complex and intricate skinning work to complete.

7.4.2 Save Skinning Data

As usual, I'm at a point with the smooth skinning process that I'm happy with, but the creature's skinning is not complete yet, as I'll revisit this during the deformation rig in Chapter 9. Just as a quick memory refresh, there are three ways to save skinning information in 3ds Max:

- Save as a New File.
- Use the *Skin Utilities* to extract a skin data file.
- Use the *Skin* modifier to extract a skin data file.

The choice you make here is entirely up to you; it is simply a way to keep the skinning information safe and away from the main file, which could corrupt for any number of reasons. So, just choose whichever method(s) you prefer and we can move onto the next section.

7.5 Bone Shaping

The reshaping of the creature's *Bones* is an optional step. For both Pheridan and Xilteor, I am choosing not to do any *Bone* reshaping and leaving the *Bones* in their default and generic styles. This not only saves time but as these creatures are going to behave quickly in the 3ds Max viewports, I feel that it is an unnecessary step. I've included these stages in both of the creatures purely to illustrate the best possible time to actually do any *Bone* reshaping if you would like to, or if your creature rig or production requires it.

7.6 Range of Motion File

Range of Motion files are animation data that animates our creature rigs from one extreme pose to the other. These ROM files show the full range of motion we expect our creatures to go through and stress-test our rigs and skinning deformations to make sure that what we create can actually cope with the situations they will be getting into. There are no tricks or secrets here: just animate directly on the *Bones* that we have in our creatures and make sure you hit all of those important poses and all of the extreme poses that will push our rigging and deformation skills to the limit (Figure 7.8).

Once you've completed the creation of the animation, save it out as a ROM file by using one of the following methods:

- Save out a new file.
- Save out an FBX animation file.
- Bake down the trajectories and save an animation file.

7.7 Motion Set List

Just like with the Pheridan rig, we don't actually need any *Motion Set Lists* (MSLs) created, as we are not relying on the use of a real-time engine to display our creations. However, this is the time that we would be starting to think about them

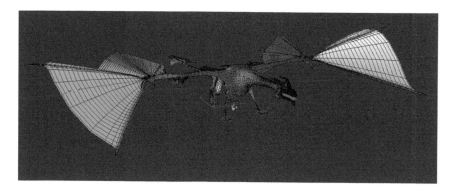

Figure 7.8

Xilteor is pushed into some pretty difficult poses which will cause troubles for both rigging and skinning deformations, but it's important that we know these things now and can adapt and create for these kinds of extremes.

if we needed to. Figure 7.9 shows my interpretation of a basic MSL for Xilteor if I were to start thinking about this creature's basic movements.

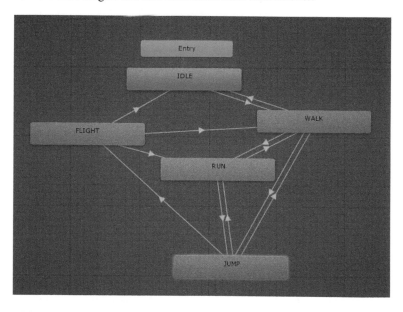

Figure 7.9

A preliminary and very basic *Motion Set List* example for Xilteor's core movements.

7.8 Controller Creation

Keeping with a similar control scheme that is featured in most rigs, we'll be using *Shapes* (*Splines*) as the basis for Xilteor's control system. By referring back to our sketches of the *Bones and Controller* layouts from Chapter 2, "The Creatures," we are able to copy the kinds of controllers we envisioned into 3ds Max. Now, we may end up adding in more controllers later, or even removing a few, but this will give us a good starting point to move on to the next stage.

I'll be going against the color conventions that we set out during Chapter 1, "Introduction," by coloring all of the controllers in a neutral gray (Figure 7.10), but I'm not forgetting about these conventions. In fact, I'll be changing out the gray to the correct color (as per the color conventions) as we work through the animation rig for Xilteor. This is going to allow me to keep a focus on things and will be a visual indicator of which controllers and sections of the rig are complete.

Figure 7.10

Xilteor's controllers have been created and placed close to where they will be used.

7.9 Summary

Xilteor now has a core hierarchical structure, a completed skeleton created with the built-in *Bones* system in 3ds Max and even has deforming geometry, as we've gone through the process of creating skin weights and skinning the creature. As the base rig forms the foundations for all other rigging layers, it has been important to get things just right. This has been and often is a time-consuming but not particularly challenging section, meaning that the base rig is exciting as it is the start of the rigging process, but is dull and boring due to the tasks assigned to it. But, fear not! The upcoming rigging stage, the animation rig, is the complete opposite. It is interesting and exciting, but difficult, technical and challenging. I like to think that one stage compensates for the other, but I'll let you make up your own mind on where you stand on this.

Onwards to the animation rig!

8

Xilteor

Animation Rig

Dragons are basically our pipe-dreams of what birds would be if they still looked liked ancient dinosaurs but followed evolution's flight plan.

Kyle Hill

This huge dragon requires a very different rigging approach to the kind of setup that we created for Pheridan. I know, Xilteor has no tentacles, but he does have a long neck and tail, so we could technically duplicate the same kind of rig that we used in the squid for these sections. However, as our main focus for this creature will be on its wings and getting it to look great flying, we can approach things in a new and exciting way.

We will start this chapter by comparing a creature named Belraus that you may already know of from the first book in this series, *Digital Creature Rigging: The Art and Science of CG Creature Setup in 3ds Max*. During this time, we will discuss the similarities and differences between these two creatures and work out what parts of the rigging systems we could recreate or what changes might work better for our dragon rig, Xilteor.

Next we will go through and create the full animation rig for our creature, using some new techniques which may give you some inspiration for what other kinds of rigging solutions may be possible. We'll finish up with a completed rig that can be used for animation and has the opportunity for further development as we move into deformations, which are covered in the following chapter.

At this point, we will be working from the following file:

- 02_CH_Xilteor_BASE.max

8.1 Xilteor vs Belraus

Way back around 2011 and 2012, Belraus, a genetically-engineered creature, was born in my imagination and in the pixelated digital three-dimensional world of 3ds Max. This creature was a mix of ideas, but generally felt like a huge dinosaur that could walk on its hands and feet like a quadruped as well as stand on its rear legs like a biped. It had some impressive features, such as the custom *Spline IK* system for the spine, stretching limbs, a face rig, the ability to have jaw dislocation just like a snake and even a muscle system. There was a lot that went into that creature, and many, if not all, of those techniques can be replicated now. So, there's the possibility that we could use some of these techniques once again.

Xilteor has many similarities to Belraus (Figure 8.1). In fact, the main body of this dragon matches the dinosaur physique and anatomy as closely as two different imaginary species could. Both stand in a quadruped position with feet and hands on the floor, both have long tails and large torsos with wide frames. Xilteor does not include the smaller arms that Belraus has, and Belraus misses out on having any kind of wings, but otherwise they are incredibly similar – even their rear legs have the same kind of *Bone* layout.

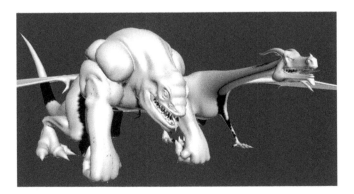

Figure 8.1

Xilteor and Belraus have some differences and many similarities. It's almost as if they were designed to live in the same make-believe universe.

8. Xilteor: Animation Rig

Technically, the exact same setup could be used for most of the Xilteor dragon rig. In fact, a setup like this would be perfect, as it is solid and performs extremely well. Additionally, if the animation team are used to how the Belraus rig controls, they will have no need to learn new controls and adjust their workflows.

So, go and recreate the same rig from the first book and we'll call this chapter complete...

...

... Only joking! Although it would make sense to recreate the same kind of setup, it would make for a boring read and we wouldn't get to experiment with other rigging methods and techniques. Of course, this doesn't mean that we can't base some of what we do on that original setup, but replicating it completely will be no fun at all. Let's experiment!

8.2 The Animation Rig

Before we start with all of the new methodologies, tricks, tips and techniques, I just want to reiterate what we just discussed. The Belraus rig that was created all those years ago can still be replicated now and will form a very solid foundation and setup for an animation team to start using. What this means is that if you and your team are comfortable with that kind of setup, then doing the same thing is not a bad thing. It actually makes the most sense. However, throughout the setup for Xilteor, we are going to focus our time on some different options and keep our minds focused on the fact that this creature rig should be designed for flight first. By thinking like this, it can and will dramatically change the areas of the setup where we will be spending most of our time.

8.2.1 Layout

The *Layout* is the top-level control for this rig and by its manipulation, it should have everything else that we create follow it. There's nothing challenging here; just make sure that the controller has its pivot located at the center of the scene. It should also be named and colored correctly and then have *Freeze Transforms* applied to it. The results of this and some other basic controls are shown in Figure 8.2.

8.2.2 Cog, Hips, Head and Tail

We're once again starting off with more very simple setups. For each of the controls, the pivot should be aligned in position to its respective *Bones* that it will control. Their pivot orientations should be aligned to the world. With these ready to go, correct naming and colors should be applied before being linked to the *Layout* controller (Figure 8.2).

We now get to make sure these controls work on the rig by using constraints. For each of the *Bones* that the control should manipulate, add a *Position Constraint* and an *Orientation Constraint* from the *Bone* to the control. If you notice any flipping, which will probably happen due to the different orientations of the *Bones* and the controls, simply make sure to check that *Keep Initial Offset* is turned on.

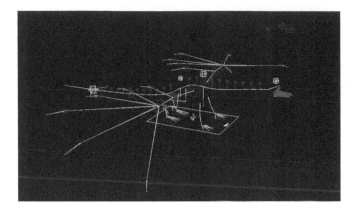

Figure 8.2

The completed Layout, COG, Hips, Head and Tail setup is quick and easy; there's nothing complicated about these starting points for the rig.

8.2.3 The Spine, Neck and Tail System

A custom *Spline IK* system is exactly what's needed here, exactly the same one that was created for the Belraus rig many years ago. There is also the option of using a trusty and basic *Forward Kinematics* system, too, or even the custom *FK* system we created for the Pheridan rig. As we're focusing more on Xilteor flying than being on the ground, we could also opt for an *Inverse Kinematics* rig, but that one is a little limiting on the overall control, as we found out when we added it to a limb from the squid. There are probably a million other options out there, too, but there's a neat system that I'd like to take you through and it can give some fluid effects for stretching and deformation… Oh, and it could even be used for tentacles, too!

This system uses geometry to control the position and orientation of *Point Helpers*, which then drive the *Bones* and skeleton that we already have in place. To start us off, we need to create some geometry; a *Plane* is best with its *Length and Width Segs* set to *1* – leaving us with a flat four-sided geometry square.

Convert the geometry into an *Editable Poly* object and align one of the edges to the head *Bone* of the creature in position only. Do the same with the opposite edge down to the neck *Bone* that is closest to the head. Keep that edge selected and shift-click and drag to clone it, creating another square of geometry. Align this new edge to the next neck *Bone* and continue this technique all the way to the end of the tail. Once finished, you should have a piece of geometry that runs from the head to the tail with edges at each one of the *Bones* in the chain (Figure 8.3).

Rename and parent this geometry into the rig, then add a *Skin* modifier to it. We are going to assign the Head control, the COG Control, the Hip control and the Tail control to the modifier instead of using *Bones*. This gives a direct connection from the controls to the geometry, and we can use standard skin weighting techniques to assign the area of effect from the controls to the plane geometry, as we see in Figure 8.4.

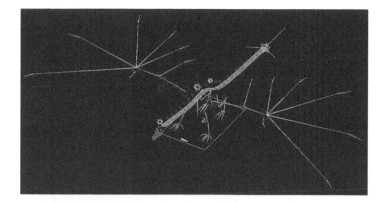

Figure 8.3

Geometry should run from the head to the tail of the creature with edges located at each of the *Bone* chain's pivots.

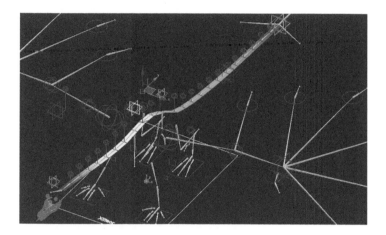

Figure 8.4

The controls of this creature are used as skin weighting influences on the geometry instead of using *Bones*.

Manipulate the controls and take your time getting that piece of geometry to move and deform as you would expect that whole central section of the creature to. After all, this is going to be what the *Bones* in the creature use to follow, position and orient themselves to.

Once you're happy with the skinning of the plane, we need to start attaching *Point Helpers* to each edge of the geometry so that we can use those for the position of each of the *Bones*. This is not a particularly difficult task to achieve, but it does require us to use a constraint this is not so often used in rigging. This constraint is the *Attachment Constraint* and it allows us to attach things directly to the faces of geometry in 3ds Max.

If you haven't used this kind of constraint before, it's better just to follow along with this example and learn all of its many nuances as you start digging into it further. So, create a *Point Helper* and add an *Attachment Constraint* from it to the geometry. This will jump that *Point Helper* over to the geometry to what will seem like a randomly assigned location. Find your *Point Helper* and manipulate one of the controls that we skinned to see how this constraint is already working.

What we need to do now is to get this *Point Helper* into a desired location, and this can all be done from the *Motion Tab* (Figure 8.5).

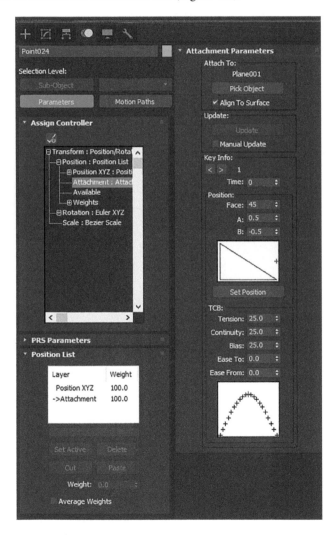

Figure 8.5

The *Motion* tab is where you can find the primary controls for the *Attachment Constraint* once it has been assigned to an object.

What's really important in this section is all of the *Position* parameters. Once you understand how all of this works, things make a lot more sense, and I suggest reading up in the help files about this modifier and just trying to use it; doing both of these things will really get you a good foundation in working with this constraint (and in most areas of 3ds Max, for that matter). For now, change the *Face* attribute to *1*, the *A* attribute to *0.5* and the *B* attribute to −0.5. You should now have the *Point Helper* sitting on an edge in the very center of the geometry. Duplicate the *Point Helper* and change the *Face* attribute until you get to the next edge. Repeat this process many times and you will be left with a geometry plane that has *Point Helpers* attached to it at every edge. Oh, and be sure to test out how these *Point Helpers* stick to their specific places by manipulating the controls that we skinned to the plane earlier (Figure 8.6).

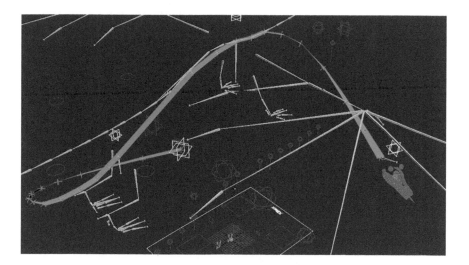

Figure 8.6

The geometry plane now has *Point Helpers* attached to it and they stay in their assigned positions even during manipulation of the controls.

All that is left to do for this setup is to get those *Bones* moving along correctly. We've actually done this kind of thing before on Pheridan, so we will use the same technique here. Each *Bone* needs to be *Position Constrained* to the *Point Helper* at its base. This will take care of its positioning. Then the *Bone* needs a *LookAt Constraint* applied to it. It should look at the *Point Helper* at the base of the next *Bone*, and its upnode should be the *Point Helper* it is *Position Constrained* to.

Creating a Custom Geometry Spine

1. Create a *Plane* in the scene.

   ```
   Create Tab > Geometry > Standard Primitives > Plane
   ```

2. Set the *Length* and *Width Segs* to *1*.

   ```
   [Select Plane] > Modify Tab > Parameters > Length Segs
   > (1)
   [Select Plane] > Modify Tab > Parameters > Width Segs >
   (1)
   ```

3. Convert to an *Editable Poly*.

   ```
   [Select Plane] > Right-Click > Convert To: > Convert to
   Editable Poly
   ```

4. Select an edge and align it to a *Bone* in position only.

5. Select the opposite edge and align it in position only to the next *Bone*.

6. Repeat this process by duplicating the edge for the full length of the *Bone* chain.

   ```
   [Select Edge] > Shift + Click & Drag
   ```

7. Create a *Point Helper* and add an *Attachment Constraint* so that it is attached to the plane.

   ```
   Create Tab > Helpers > Standard > Point[Select Point
   Helper] > Animation Menu > Constraints > Attachment
   Constraint
   ```

8. Set the *Face* parameter to *1*.

   ```
   [Select Point Helper] > Motion Tab > Attachment
   Parameters > Position > Face
   ```

9. Set the *A* and *B* attributes to *0.5* and *−0.5*, respectively.

   ```
   [Select Point Helper] > Motion Tab > Attachment
   Parameters > Position > A
   [Select Point Helper] > Motion Tab > Attachment
   Parameters > Position > B
   ```

10. Duplicate the *Point Helper* and change the *Face* parameter as required. Continue this step for all edges/*Bones*.

11. Add a *Position Constraint* from the *Bone* to its *Point Helper*.

    ```
    Animation Menu > Constraints > Position Constraint
    ```

12. Add a *LookAt Constraint* from the *Bone* to the next *Point Helper*.

    ```
    Animation Menu > Constraints > LookAt Constraint
    ```

13. Set the upnode as its own *Point Helper* that it is *Position Constrained* to.

    ```
    [Select Object] > Motion Tab > PRS Parameters >
    Rotation > LookAt Constraint > Select Upnode
    ```

14. Repeat for all *Bones* in the chain.

Once all of the *Bones* have *Position* and *LookAt Constraints* correctly set, this part of the rig should be mostly complete (Figure 8.7). Next up, we just need to link the controls together. The hip and COG need to be linked to the Torso control; then link the Torso, Head and Tail to the Body control and everything should be

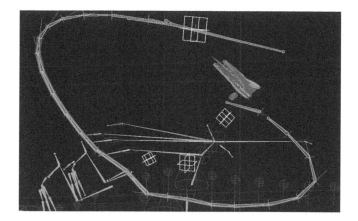

Figure 8.7

The completed system gives a different option when we think about controls and setups for the central sections of our creatures.

great. This not only puts the controls in a neat hierarchy but also give us a lot of control over the various parts of the dragon, which will be very important when we animate it flying.

As always, look for colors and naming as well as making sure things are sitting correctly in the hierarchy before moving on – that pretty much wraps up things here.

8.2.4 Tail Fin

If you look into the *Bones* that are in the tail fin, you will notice two *Bones* additionally in there, one for each side. I'm not adding any control into these, and I've decided that any additional deformation in this area is not really needed. Now, I had the option to remove these completely, and I would do this if working in a production environment. However, I figured that this would be a good thing to leave in and explain, as things don't always go to plan, and as this is not an exact science (or even close to scientific); things sometimes just don't work out as we would expect them to. Trial and error plays a big part in the rigging process as well as testing and experimentation – or maybe they both mean the same thing, but one sounds more professional?!

Anyway, there are additional *Bones* in there and please feel free to use them if you would like to. Alternatively, you could go in there and remove them and add in your own rigging solution. But, whatever you choose to do, just remember that if this is not going to be the main focus of the creature, a simpler solution and output may be the best option and our time could be spent better elsewhere.

8.2.5 Front Arms

We're not going to get too fancy with these front arms (or legs if you prefer), and we're going to rely on some basic *IK* chains to do the majority of the work for us.

We're also not worrying about stretching, as all of these more complex setups were covered in the first *Digital Creature Rigging* book and reiterating all of that is just no fun at all.

So, grab yourself an *IK* solver and run it from the top of the arm to the hand and add another *IK* for the hand. As usual, I'm using *HI Solvers* for these and nothing else. Parent these up to the hand control and assign the elbow control as the pole vector for the arm.

With the arm and hand fixed up properly, we're using straightforward *Orientation Constraints* from the *Bones* to their respective controls for each of the finger *Bones*. Finish things up by using a *Point Constraint* on the uppermost arm *Bone* to the shoulder control to give some extra options for movement. All of these procedures are not new to us, so I won't give a step-by-step breakdown here, but you can refer to other areas in this book for guides that show you how all of this works if you need a recap on anything. This completes the arms of the creature (Figure 8.8).

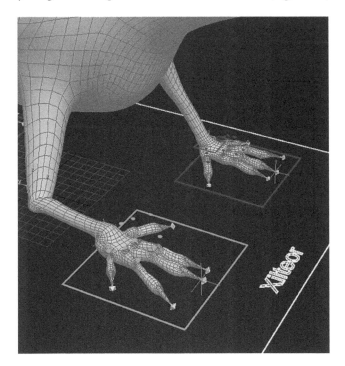

Figure 8.8

The arms of Xilteor are a simple setup that relies on just *IK* and *Orientation Constraints*.

8.2.6 Rear Legs

The rear legs of Xilteor are a very close match to the of the Belraus creature, and the exact same setup can be transferred to this rig completely, including the overlapping

IK method. This method combines two *IK* chains into the leg due to the scissorlike style of the creature. We first need to create an *HI Solver IK* chain from the upper leg *Bone* to the middle or third *Bone* in the chain and then another *IK* from the second *Bone* to the fourth *Bone*, which should look something like Figure 8.9.

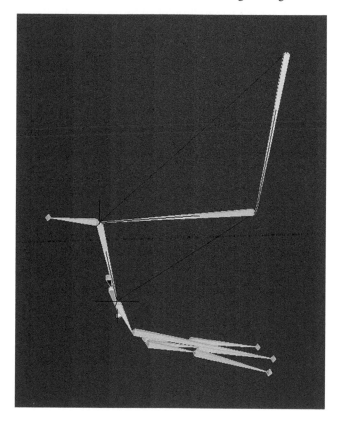

Figure 8.9

Overlapping *IK Solvers* are unorthodox, but, used correctly, can achieve desirable results quickly and easily.

Parent both of the *IK* chains into the foot control and only assign the knee control to the pole vector target of the uppermost *IK* chain. If you manipulate the foot or knee control, you should now have good movement in the rear leg. All that's left to do is use *Orientation Constraints* for the foot and toe controllers, similarly to how we did things for the fingers.

8.2.7 Dragon Wings

There are so many options for us to consider when it comes to rigging in general, and wings, dragon wings or other, are no exception. In fact, just like the tentacles of Pheridan, we are able to use multiple setups for the wings and combine them into one rig if we really want to. Alternatively, we could create shot-specific rigs instead, which would allow us to really focus on specific aspects of the wing rigging. Whatever we choose, the one thing that always stays the same is the need for a solid setup that animators are happy to use.

This brings us to the actual building of the wing rigs, and for Xilteor we are going to create a basic setup that can support up to three very different kinds of rigs. What this will mean is that the setup will contain a complex hierarchy that will allow the three setups to function both independently and together. However, we will build just the manual animation rig during this chapter and, just like we did with the Pheridan rig, we will have a shot-specific rig, or two of them in this case, to look into during the following chapter.

8.2.7.1 Foundations of a Multilayered Wing Rig: Hierarchy and Manual Animation Inputs

Setting up the manual animation rig for the wings of Xilteor could be incredibly simple. After all, if we just want rotational controls, then it's a simple case of linking *FK*-style controls together and using constraints to get them to control the *Bones* of the creature. If *IK*-style control is desired, then the same controls could be used, but the *Bones* could have an *IK solver* attached to them. Both of these solutions can be perfect to work with: they're quick and simple to set up while being quick and simple to work with. If this is all you need, then go for it; there really is no need to overcomplicate things… But for this book, this kind of rudimentary setup might make for a boring read, so we are going to extend this setup into something a little more challenging.

The aims of the wing rig for Xilteor include the following:

- The systems have to be standalone and not interfere with the rest of the creature's rig.
- There should be a single control which automatically folds the wings based on predefined poses and controller positions.
- Included in the setup must be an automated wing flapping solution which does not require keyframes or manual animation of any kind.
- A complete manual control system relying on *Forward Kinematics* controls that allow for all kinds of movements for both of the wings.
- All *FK* controls should follow any other setups and movements that we create while being able to offset and/or add to any automated motion that we assign to the wings.

That's five big points that we need to get into our rigging solution, and although it may seem like a big task, most of this will come down to some clever hierarchy linking. Actually, as the hierarchical structure is so important, that's where we are going to spend most of our time right now.

As we've done many times before, we will be enlisting the use of many *Point Helpers* in this crazy hierarchy setup. Due to this, there really isn't any kind of

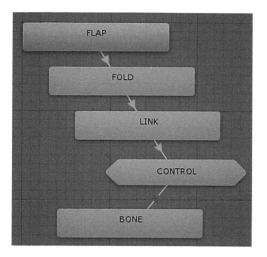

Figure 8.10

The hierarchy of the wings might seem complicated at first, but it is really just a way of allowing one *Point Helper* to control another, giving multiple options for the wing's manipulation.

step-by-step guide that I could include that would make much sense. In fact, a text breakdown of the hierarchy and a clever diagram might make much more sense.

Although it's relatively simple at its core, things might seem complicated on a first look, but Figure 8.10 includes a visual explanation of exactly what's going on in this hierarchy structure. We're basically putting multiple *Point Helpers* in a hierarchy and allowing one to control another, giving us multiple layers of control, as described below:

- XILTEOR MAIN HIERARCHY: The main hierarchy for the Xilteor dragon creature. This includes all parts of the creature and controllers.
    - FLAP Locator (*Point Helper*): The FLAP locators form the base node for both of the wings. It is these *Point Helpers* that will be used to control the automated flapping of the wings. Every other locator will follow this motion.
        - FOLD Locator (*Point Helper*): Sitting below the automated flapping are the locators that control the automated folding of the wings. The folds will be created manually by us and are then stored in a single attribute that can be blended in and out of.
            - LINK Locator (*Point Helper*): The final locator is used only for linking the controller into this folding and flapping hierarchy. It acts as a buffer between the controller and the automation and is there as a safety net in case we need any additional controls that we may have overlooked.

- CTRL (Controller): Last but not least is the actual controller that we can use for manual animation. What's great about the controllers being at the end of this hierarchy is that they will take any movement from the automated locators, meaning that they stay in place no matter what is happening to the wing rig. We lose the ability to double-click and select the full *FK* controls, but it's a small price to pay for the kind of great setup that this allows us to achieve.

Even with this setup in place, things won't work until we add *Position and Orientation Constraints* to the *Bones* that will be controlled by the controllers. There's nothing new here, so just go ahead and add them. Things for this setup should technically be complete and we'll look into the automation elements during the next chapter. Xilteor's wings should now be fully controlled by the controllers and even react when we manipulate any of the *Point Helpers* we added to this setup while the controllers follow along (Figure 8.11).

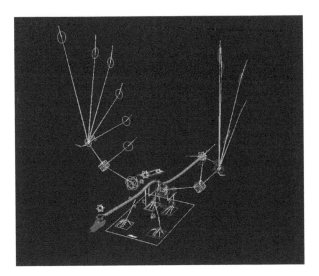

Figure 8.11

The completed wing setup allows the controllers to follow along with any manipulations made to the FLAP and FOLD locators. It also allows us to additively manipulate the wings using those same controllers.

8.3 Summary

This concludes the creation of the animation rig for Xilteor the dragon. During this setup we've used some common and familiar methods and expanded on those by using lesser-used and lesser-known techniques for areas like the spine, neck and tail sections. We then looked into a more complicated hierarchy setup in order to give us a lot of options for controlling the wings of the creature. By including this larger hierarchy with multiple locators, we have built the foundations on which we are able to add automation and additional movement to the creature without disturbing the basic *Forward Kinematic* controls. In fact, we've built this in such a way that any automation we actually add to the rig will allow the *FK* controllers to follow along with the movement and even enable us to have additive control over the full motion. We'll discuss all of the automation setups in the next chapter, and we will even look at adding automatic overlapping action into the wings, too.

9

Xilteor

Deformation Rig

So comes snow after fire, and even dragons have their ending!

J. R. R. Tolkien

Not including the interesting neck/spine/tail setup and a complicated wing hierarchy, the animation rig for Xilteor is relatively basic. But, as our core focus for this creature is on its flying, we have an opportunity to really focus on the elements that are important for that very specific purpose. The most obvious areas that affect the creature's flight are its wings, and during this chapter we'll be looking into the automation of two important movements that this creature needs to accomplish – the flapping and folding of the wings.

Before we jump into the wings of this creature, we will take a look over any extra sections that we may be missing and add them to the rig. From there we'll review the deformations of the creature and finish everything by adding some automatic overlapping action as an additional visual technique for this rig.

To follow along, open the following file:

- 03_CH_Xilteor_RIG.max

9.1 Face Lift

When we created the rig for this creature, we really neglected the face and any facial features completely. This is a good point to rectify that, and for the uses of Xilteor, we don't need to add too many complexities to the face rig at all.

The first thing that we should really tackle is the jaw and tongue of the creature. We can copy the exact same rig that was used for Belraus in the first *Digital Creature Rigging* book, as the dislocated jaw with control over its shape would work perfectly. However, Xilteor really doesn't need those kinds of control, so I'm going with a single jaw *Bone* with around four *Bones* for the tongue. This will allow us a good amount of control over the tongue geometry and make opening and closing the jaw a simple process, as both of these setups will work on *FK* rotations only (Figure 9.1).

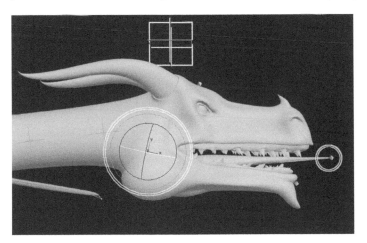

Figure 9.1

The jaw and tongue setup for Xilteor contains a basic *FK* rotation to get the amount of control that is needed.

As usual, the *skinning* for this setup takes the most time. Controls are simple spline shapes, just like we've used for the rest of the creature's rig. I've attached the tongue to the jaw and the jaw to the head to make sure that the hierarchy for this part of the creature stays in a logical way.

Although there is a lot of opportunity to add many options to the facial controls for Xilteor, I'm going to take the same approach that we did for Pheridan. What approach, you ask? Well, that's adding a blink control to the head and using a *Morpher* modifier to enable a single morph target. The procedure is just the same as before; we need to duplicate the geometry, edit it and feed it into the *Morpher* modifier channel at *100.0* and turn on *Automatically Reload Targets* to enable us to see any changes that have been made. I'm guessing that for such a straightforward setup that a step-by-step guide is overkill, and if you do need to refresh your memory, just head over to Chapter 6, "Pheridan: Deformation Rig," for all the details that you'll need.

9.2 Cleaning the Geometric Deformations

Xilteor is a solid rig already, but there are areas of the geometry where the deformations could be improved. Just manipulating the controls of the creature can help us identify areas which could use a little more help and attention, especially in those areas that have stretching or geometry that closely overlaps. Unfortunately for this model, our main troublesome areas seem to be the chest, spine and hip areas and the wings (Figure 9.2).

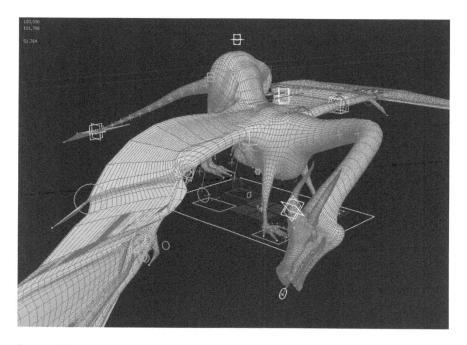

Figure 9.2

Xilteor deforms great for the most part, but the chest, spine and hips have troubles when stretching, and the wings are plagued by close geometry that overlaps when manipulated.

The chest, spine and hip areas are closely related and affect one another under movement in the central spine area. We could start to look into *Pose-Space Deformations*, which are an advanced form of the *Morpher* modifier called the *Skin Morph* modifier. However, with some adjustments to the skinning weights we already created, we can eliminate most of the problems and have a creature rig that should deform well enough for most of its needs.

Sadly, the wings are a whole lot of trouble. They have what is known as nonuniform overlapping geometry (Figure 9.3), or at least that's what I'm calling it. What this means is that there are two sides to the model, closely positioned together, but their edges and vertices do not match. If geometry is placed closely

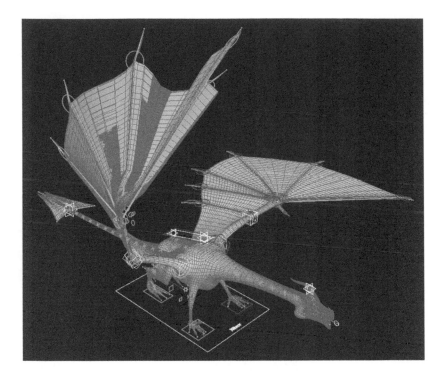

Figure 9.3

The nonuniform overlapping geometry on the wings of the Xilteor creature causes us a number of problems as they deform, and unfortunately this is an area of the creature that is easily seen and will have motion applied to it.

together, it is incredibly important to have the edges and vertices match, as it allows for us to skin exactly the same on both sides. This eliminates the chances of the geometry penetrating through and overlapping during movement. This is not important for nondeforming geometry, but when it comes to flesh-surface deformations and characters and creatures in particular, it is incredibly important.

The best solution, and really the only solution that you should consider, is to send this back to modeling and have things fixed up correctly. However, this is not always possible due to production deadlines and project constraints, so there are times when we just have to deal with the thing, no matter how troublesome it may be. We're at this point with Xilteor right now. We've nearly completed the rigging for this creature and our modeling team has already left the building, so it is up to us to fix things.

Our first option is to go ahead and fix the geometry, but this may cause big trouble for others in your team (if you're working in a production). For instance, the surfacing and shading teams may already have this model, and edits to the geometry will affect *UVs* and texture coordinates, amongst other things like vertex numbering and normals. Really, the worst thing that we could do would

9. Xilteor: Deformation Rig

be to cause problems for someone else, so maybe fixing the geometry ourselves is not the best idea... I understand that these kinds of thoughts and planning are not needed if you're working on your own, but it's something to keep in mind when moving into production if you're not there already.

There are other possible solutions to the wing issues, of course. We could look into *Pose-Space Deformations*, but it may be better to add these after animation so that we can see the actual problems with the deformations instead of trying to guess them. Additionally, waiting until after the animation is complete to add these *PSDs* will mean that our rigs are kept clean and perform as quickly as possible in the viewports.

Other options could include adding various modifiers to the geometry or just the affected areas. Things like the *Push* modifier may help to pull apart the geometry in some troublesome poses, which is a quick-fix solution, but I have a feeling this would only be suitable for the smallest geometry penetration issues. The *Relax* modifier may also be of assistance in relaxing the geometry instead of pushing it, but your mileage may vary on both of these options.

You may not even have to worry about this at all. If you're planning on using something complex for some of the wing deformations, any geometry penetration might not even be a problem. Oh, and what I'm talking about here are things like adding *Cloth* to deform the geometry automatically as it is moved. Sure, the main areas of the wings which have *Bones* to control and deform them will still have to be fixed if there are problems, but areas which have automatic overlapping action and are affected by computational deformers like cloth will not have troubles with overlapping geometry. This is purely because deformers like cloth are calculated after animation is applied and often have their own attributes, parameters and settings that control penetrations, and so on.

Xilteor really needs some extra attention here, and we can start by focusing on the skinning deformations and weights that we already have in our *Skin* modifier. From there we can use any of the techniques mentioned above to try to fix things the best that we possibly can. As the geometry does have some fundamental issues to begin with, we may have to rely on fixing things after shots and sequences have been animated. This is not ideal, but it is a true-to-life production style where things don't always go according to plan!

9.3 Wing Automation Controls

With the focus of the Xilteor creature being mostly on his ability to fly and soar through the air, the wings of this creature have become probably the most important element. During Chapter 8, "Xilteor – Animation Rig," we actually created a specific hierarchy using many *Point Helpers* which will allow us to add a number of automated animations to the creature. These automated animations give us the opportunity to explore and experiment with some more advanced rigging topics as well as giving the animators and other users of our rig the chance to try out some amazing automated animation controls.

Now we already have the *FK* controls built into our wing rigs. This means that we are able to manipulate and animate the wings currently, but as these controls are attached in a clever system of hierarchical goodness, we can add in automation without disturbing any of those controllers. In fact, we can even enhance those existing controllers as they will follow along with our additional automation and be able to push movement and animation into those additively. It's pretty cool.

9.3.1 Automated Flapping

I've been trying my very best to keep calculations and any kind of math to an absolute minimum throughout this book. However, it's no real secret that what we do all the time during rigging is to calculate various things. In fact, automatically getting the wings of this dragon to flap could easily be done using trigonometry and expressions – in particular by using sine waves, amplitude, time, period and a host of other mathematical mumbo-jumbo... It's not actually that difficult overall, but it's not my idea of fun, usually!

Anyway, so with all of that said, is there an easy way to get these wings to flap automatically and without using math? Well, no there isn't. Not really. So does that mean we're going to be doing mathematics now? Actually, no. We don't have to.

There is a built-in *rotation controller* that we can use to do all of the math for us and make the automated flapping a simple task to set up. This is actually a really great way of doing things, but there is one drawback that may make you want to stop and think before adding this solution to your rigs. You see, this rotation controller has all of the great stuff already added to it, but to access that great stuff, we need to always find the controller in 3ds Max. That's right, there is no actual way of accessing any of the attributes or parameters of this controller without finding it – sadly, another limitation of 3ds Max.

Okay, so what's all this great stuff I'm talking about and what is the actual controller? What I'm talking about is the *Waveform Float*. It has everything we need to create automatically flapping wings with no mathematics needed by us, as the controller takes care of everything.

Grab hold of the first FLAP locator, which should have control over all of the other locators and controls for the wing, as it is top in the hierarchy. Then, with the locator selected, navigate to the rotation controllers for this object. You should be able to select a specific *rotation axis* (we are working with *Y and Z rotations* for Xilteor's wings) and change it out to this *Waveform Float*, which will open a new window with all of the controls that we need in there already created for us, as shown in Figure 9.4.

Press play to view the animation that has been automatically created. It may not look right just yet, but there's definitely something happening! When the *Waveform Float* has been applied to the first FLAP locator, we need to adjust some of the settings for it to work correctly. In particular, I'm focusing on just two of the parameters in this window, *Period* and *Amplitude*. Editing either

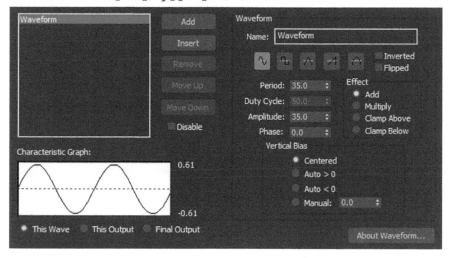

Figure 9.4

The *Waveform Float* rotation controller includes everything that we need to create automatically flapping wings in a new comprehensive window.

of these attributes will change the style of flapping that this has given to the wing, so it's worth playing with these to see what you like best. Make sure to add another one of these modifiers to the other rotation axis so that they are applied to the Y and Z axes for this locator. Then adjust the parameters as needed and required. Here are the settings which I found appealing for Xilteor's wing flapping:

- Y Rotation Axis
  - Period: 00000.0
  - Amplitude: 00000.0
- Z Rotation Axis
  - Period: 00000.0
  - Amplitude: 00000.0

To finish up this setup, I went ahead and wired the rotations of the first FLAP locator to the second and third in its chain. This allows us to duplicate the rotations of the first locator automatically to the rest, giving a more believable and realistic automated flapping.

It's really incredible what this controller can do, but I have to warn you once again that the only way to edit the parameters of this is to find it manually in your scene. You can't even animate its parameters, so it's great if you need the dragon

Automated Flapping Using a Waveform Float Rotation Controller

1. Select the uppermost FLAP locator and add a *Waveform Float* controller to its *Y Rotation*.

    ```
    [Select Object] > Motion Tab > Parameters > Assign
    Controller > Rotation > Y Rotation > Assign Controller
    > Waveform Float
    ```

2. Adjust the *Period* parameter.

    ```
    Waveform Controller Window > Waveform > Period
    ```

3. Adjust the *Amplitude* parameter.

    ```
    Waveform Controller Window > Waveform > Amplitude
    ```

4. Repeat steps 1, 2 and 3 for the *Z Rotation*.

5. Wire the rotations of the other FLAP locators so that they rotate with the same values.

to continuously flap, but if you want to go from static to flapping and back again, well, it's not so great. But hey, no math!

If you notice that the wings do not sync correctly, then you may need to turn on the *Inverted* and/or *Flipped* parameters in the *Waveform* controller window by clicking the checkboxes. This will keep the rest of the settings exactly the same but invert or flip the calculations so that they match up correctly. To turn off the automatic flapping, simply change the following attributes to the numbers shown and the wings will stay at their default positions:

- Period: 0.01
- Amplitude: 0.0

9.3.2 Automated Folding

The automatic folding of the wings is something that we have complete control over while we set this up. You see, right now, if we rotate the wing controls, we can get the wings into a folded position pretty easily and we can even animate this folding in the usual way that we animate anything in 3ds Max.

What's great about our hierarchical setup for these wings is that we can do the exact same thing to the FOLD locators. So, instead of animating on the actual controls which animators would use, we drop into the hierarchy and find the FOLD locators, set a keyframe on them in their open position and then animate them closing and folding into a position that is visually appealing. We then simply store the open and folded wing positions into a custom attribute by way of the *Reaction Manager* and *Reaction Controller* (Figure 9.5).

The methods that we use for this wing setup, in combination with clever hierarchy systems, offer many fantastic kinds of controls. In fact, this exact method could even be used for more complicated movements, like something

Using the Reaction Manager to Create an Automated Wing Folding Attribute and Controller

1. Turn on *Auto Key*.
   ```
   Animation and Time Controls > Auto Key Animation Mode
   ```
2. Select all of the wing FOLD locators and set a *Key* at *frame 0*.
   ```
   [Select Objects > Animation and Time Controls > Set
   Keys (K)
   ```
3. With the FOLD locators still selected, move the *Time Slider* to *frame 100* and set another *Key*. We now have animation on our FOLD locators, but as there are no changes in transformations, nothing is going to happen just yet.
4. With the *Time Slider* still at *frame 100*, use rotations to get the wing into a closed position that you are happy with.
5. When you've finished animating and the movement from the wing open (*frame 0*) to the wing closed (*frame 100*) looks great, then turn off *Auto Key*.
   ```
   Animation and Time Controls > Auto Key Animation Mode
   ```
6. Add an *Attribute Holder* to the controller you would like to add a custom attribute to that will control the wing folding.
   ```
   [Select Object] > Modify Tab > Modifier List > Attribute
   Holder
   ```
7. Add a *Float Slider* custom attribute that ranges *From 0.0 To 100.0* with a *Default of 0.0*. Make sure its name is something logical like "Fold." This will be used as the controller for the folding of the wing.
   ```
   Animation Menu > Parameter Editor… Alt+1
   ```
8. Open the *Reaction Manager*.
   ```
   Animation Menu > Reaction Manager
   ```
9. Add the *Float Slider* as the *Master*.
10. Select all of the FOLD locators and use the *Add Selected* button to add their *X, Y* and *Z rotations* in this *Reaction* setup. These are what will be driven from our custom attribute.
11. Create a *State* for this *Reaction*. The wings should be open as the *Slider* is set to *0.0*.
12. Create another *State*; this time, the wings should be in their folded position and the *Slider* should be set to *100.0*.
13. Wire the custom attribute to the *Reaction* controller to enable the attribute to control the movements.
14. You now have a custom attribute that can open and fold the wing automatically. Repeat this process for the wing on the opposite side.

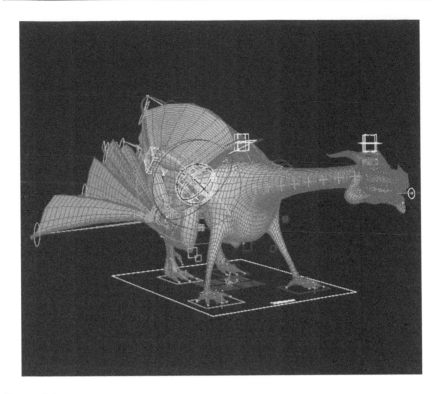

Figure 9.5

The automated folding of the wings is stored in a custom attribute that was created in conjunction with the *Reaction Manager.*

transforming and shape-shifting into something else. For these more advanced movements and changes, we simply add more keyframes to our original animation and make sure to create a *State* for each keyframe as the custom attribute runs from the start of its range until its end. This can often take a lot of time to get right, but once you have it locked down, it's almost as if you can magically store animation into a controller (Figure 9.6)... And you kind of do, especially if you get an animator to animate things first and then use that data to store into the custom attribute. Amazing things can happen when working with this kind of technique.

9.3.3 Automatic Overlapping Action

The wing rig is great as it is already. We have an automated system that we can adjust as we need it for the wings to automatically flap slowly and quickly and as much as we need them to. There is also a built-in automated folding system that is hooked up to a custom attribute for direct control. Then we have manual animation controls that not only give us direct access to all parts of the wing but also follow along with the movements from our automated setups so that

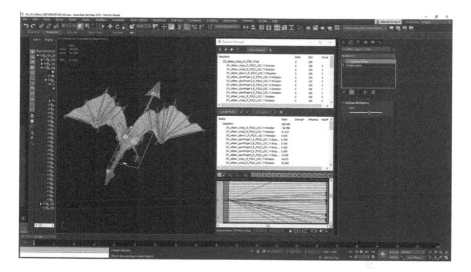

Figure 9.6

Animation (really just keyframes) is stored magically in the *Reaction Manager* and custom *Slider* attribute that we created.

we can additively animate on top of all of this great stuff we have going on in this rig. But, you know what? We can add just one more thing that will make this even better.

To include *overlapping action* into our wing rig, an animator could go ahead and actually physically animate that themselves. And honestly, for many of the shots that this creature may be used for, that is exactly what will happen. This isn't a bad thing at all, as it gives the animator complete control over the look and feel of the motion that they are applying to the rig. However, there may be times when getting this overlapping action for free may be beneficial. I'm thinking of times when the creature is idle and just hovering in the air, so the automatic wing flapping could be used along with automated overlapping action which we can add. This might also be helpful if the creature is just flying throughout a shot and there are more important areas for animation to focus on, or there just isn't enough time for the animation team to get in there and animate this thing fully. This happens at times, and we can make things easier for everyone by adding in this kind of automated movement and control.

Actually, let's add this automatic overlapping action in as an extra and not into part of the main rig. What I mean by this is that we "wing it." No naming, no thinking about hierarchies, no working this into the main rig setup that we have. We'll bolt this onto the wing as if we needed to just add this in quickly into a shot that's already in production. Exciting!

First thing we need for this to work is a *Line* drawn from the third wing control to each of the fingers, through to the elbow and finishing at the shoulder. Figure 9.7 can illustrate this better than I can explain it in text.

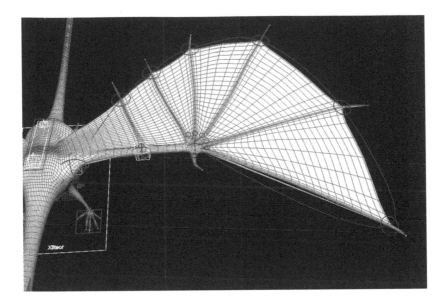

Figure 9.7

A *Line* needs to run from the third wing control through the fingers and elbow back to the shoulder of the creature.

Creating Automatic Overlapping Action for the Creature's Wings

1. Create a *Line* from the third wing controller through the fingers to the elbow and finishing at the shoulder.
   ```
   Create Tab > Shapes > Splines > Line
   ```
2. Add a *Spline IK* modifier to the *Line*.
   ```
   [Select Object] > Modify Tab > Modifier List > Spline
   IK Control
   ```
3. Create *Helpers* for this modifier with the *No Linking* parameter selected.
4. Parent the *Helpers* to the wing controls.
   ```
   Main Toolbar > Select and Link
   ```
5. Add a *Spring* controller to the position controllers of each of the *Helpers*.
   ```
   [Select Object] > Motion Tab > Assign Controller >
   Position > Assign Controller > Spring
   ```
6. Adjust the *Drag* parameter to adapt the automatic overlapping action effects.

9. Xilteor: Deformation Rig

This *Line* needs a *Spline IK* modifier added to it and *Helpers* that have *No Linking* assigned to it. These newly created *Helpers* need to be parented into the controller that they sit next to, so the shoulder *Helper* to the shoulder control, the elbow *Helper* to the elbow control, and so on. This will make the line follow along with any motion that the wing has, no matter if that movement is hand-keyed or automated.

Next we need to add *Springs* to the *Helpers* that were created on the *Line*. This is going to give the dampening that we need so that the *Line* will follow the wing's motion, but take extra frames to get there – giving the illusion of overlapping action. Each of the *Springs* that we add needs to have different *Drag* attributes attached to it, but this is something that you can experiment with to get the look that you desire.

The final step is to use *LookAt* constraints on the *Bones* so that they aim towards their respective *Helper* objects. You need to watch that *upnode* as always, but this requires very little time to set up, and the results are completely worth it (Figure 9.8).

Figure 9.8

It's a quick process to create great automatic overlapping action for the wings of this creature, which makes a huge difference to the visuals when the wings move. As we added this on top of the main rig, this technique can be used as and when we need it.

9.4 Summary

There are still some issues with the deformations of the Xilteor creature – I know, I'm aware of it! The thing is, the solutions to fix these problems up are explained in this book, many of the techniques are shown in the first *Digital Creature Rigging* book and I really didn't want to focus on the same stuff that we have discussed previously. My apologies if this is troubling, but you can really fix all of the geometry issues by following the advice in this book and just working through it.

Instead of just fixes, we used this chapter to add some rudimentary face controls which include a blink, the jaw and tongue for this creature. We then spent the rest of our time looking into tips, tricks, techniques and methods that we can use to automate some of the features of the wing rigs. We end this chapter with a completed rig which has automatic flapping (without the need for us to do any math), a control that automatically folds the wings into a great-looking position and we even created a bolt-on rig that creates automatic overlapping action on top of any wing motion. Oh, and those manual animation controls still work even after all of those additions. Now that's a pretty great place to be to finish out this rig.

10

Conclusion

One approaches the journey's end. But the end is a goal, not a catastrophe.

George Sand

With this, the final chapter of this book, we are at the conclusion and the end of our *Digital Creature Rigging* journey. It's at this point where we discuss what we've created and recap the tools, tips, tricks, techniques and methodologies that we have used throughout the creation of the creature rigs... At least, that's what usually happens and what I've done in books I've written before. But we're going to break out from that bubble.

Throughout this chapter, we're going to discuss the included files, which you can download from the companion website (www.digitalrigging.com), and we will look into the creation of the cover image that was created using the exact same files that are available to you via download. I'd like to take a moment to chat about *Digital Creature Rigging* and the two-book legacy that will be forever printed on these pages, or printed digitally, or just forgotten in a library somewhere or on a bookshelf – I want to talk about it no matter where this eventually ends up!

I would also like to mention another book that is not part of this collection, but uses the same basic principles to allow us to create rigs for mechanical creations.

After all of that, I'd like to wrap things up with a personal message and some thoughts on your next steps. I hope you'll find this chapter as interesting as the others. Let's move forward!

10.1 Things Should Be Cleaner Than This

Throughout all of the rigging and setups that we created, there is one area which was neglected throughout this book and that is the clean-up on the rig files. Things might work correctly and everything looks great on the surface, but even just a few seconds with the rigs and you might notice a few things which could be cleaned up. I'll not go into details on what should be automatic for you as an amazing rigging person, but as a quick checklist, you could look into the following things to clean the rigs up a little bit:

- Locking object controls that aren't needed or should not be touched.
- Making sure that *Freeze Transformations* have been correctly applied and applying them if not.
- Hiding items that should not be seen in the viewports.
- Adding objects into the correct *Display Layers*.
- Naming all objects logically.

10.2 Congratulations

I nearly forgot to say – CONGRATULATIONS!

You have successfully gone through all of the chapters in this book and created two very different creature rigs that are ready for production. In addition to that, we went through and used some techniques that may be unorthodox and less well known, but ended up creating some amazing automatic movements that can help to enhance other rigs that we may be working on in the future.

It's not always easy finding guides on the more complicated areas of rigging in 3D, but I hope that the solutions that we covered throughout this book will be helpful for you. If you're able to just take even a tiny amount of the methods used in these pages and apply them to other rigs, you will have already increased your own personal rigging toolset. That's pretty awesome, and you should be very proud of yourself.

10.3 File Breakdowns

We managed to create a number of different files as we worked through the rigs for the two creatures. I did point out which files we were using for each chapter and even during some specific sections, but I thought it might be a good idea to include a section here that can act as a quick reference guide if you would like dissect things or just grab hold of them for testing and reference purposes (Figure 10.1).

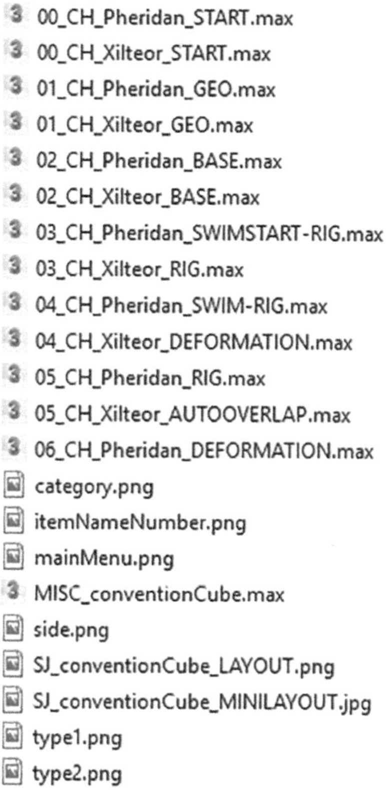

3   00_CH_Pheridan_START.max
3   00_CH_Xilteor_START.max
3   01_CH_Pheridan_GEO.max
3   01_CH_Xilteor_GEO.max
3   02_CH_Pheridan_BASE.max
3   02_CH_Xilteor_BASE.max
3   03_CH_Pheridan_SWIMSTART-RIG.max
3   03_CH_Xilteor_RIG.max
3   04_CH_Pheridan_SWIM-RIG.max
3   04_CH_Xilteor_DEFORMATION.max
3   05_CH_Pheridan_RIG.max
3   05_CH_Xilteor_AUTOOVERLAP.max
3   06_CH_Pheridan_DEFORMATION.max
🖼   category.png
🖼   itemNameNumber.png
🖼   mainMenu.png
3   MISC_conventionCube.max
🖼   side.png
🖼   SJ_conventionCube_LAYOUT.png
🖼   SJ_conventionCube_MINILAYOUT.jpg
🖼   type1.png
🖼   type2.png

Figure 10.1

There are a number of files for each of the creatures which are included with the resources download.

As always, these files are available online at www.DigitalRigging.com. Let's take a look at what they are and what they include:

- CONVENTION CUBE
  - MISC_conventionCube.max
    - This file contains the convention cube to be used as digital reference for the naming conventions that we use for these creature rigs.
  - Category.png
  - itemNameNumber.png
  - mainMenu.png
  - side.png
  - type1.png
  - type2.png

- These six image files include information on the naming conventions. They are the same images that appear on each side of the cube.
- SJ_conventionCube_LAYOUT.png
- SJ_conventionCube_MINILAYOUT.png
  - These two images are of the net of the convention cube. They can be printed, cut, folded and stuck so that you can have a physical convention cube at your desk and in the office.
- PHERIDAN
  - 00_CH_Pheridan_START.max
    - We start off the Pheridan creature rigging process with this file. It contains the geometry for this creature, but it is not cleaned or in any kind of hierarchy, but rigs have to start somewhere, right?!
  - 01_CH_Pheridan_GEO.max
    - Our next file includes the geometry once again, but this time it has been cleaned and put into a basic hierarchy. Additionally, *Display Layers* have been created, although the objects in the scene have not been properly assigned.
  - 02_CH_Pheridan_BASE.max
    - Pheridan's base rig file includes a clean hierarchy which has *Bones* and skinning information. There are also controllers added to this scene, and they are there for reference and can be used in your setups if required.
  - 03_CH_Pheridan_SWIMSTART-RIG.max
    - This file includes the fully rigged upper section of Pheridan with the limbs ready for rigging.
  - 04_CH_Pheridan_SWIM-RIG.max
    - This is the automated swimming rig for this squid creature. It allows you to view the finished automation rig, which includes both the swimming and automatic overlapping action components.
  - 05_CH_Pheridan_RIG.max
    - This is the finished animation rig which can be used for manual animation. There are no automated sections added into this rig.
  - 06_CH_Pheridan_DEFORMATION.max
    - The final Pheridan file includes some added modifiers and deformers for your exploration.
- XILTEOR
  - 00_CH_Xilteor_START.max
    - The starting point for the Xilteor dragon creature is similar to Pheridan's. Geometry is included in this file but needs a lot of work!
  - 01_CH_Xilteor_GEO.max
    - The geometry file for this creature includes cleaned geometry in a basic hierarchy with *Display Layers* included but not set.
  - 02_CH_Xilteor_BASE.max

- A clean hierarchy with bones and skinning data included with the base file. This is a good starting point for all rigging tasks.
- 03_CH_Xilteor_RIG.max
  - The Xilteor rig file has a complete creature rig for manual animation.
- 04_CH_Xilteor_DEFORMATION.max
  - This deformation file includes all of the features from the earlier rig file but also includes all automated inputs. These include both the automatic flapping movement as well as fully folding wings via a custom attribute setup.
- 05_CH_Xilteor_AUTOOVERLAP.max
  - Xilteor's final file includes a demonstration of what is possible using this additional setup that can be bolted on to control automatic overlapping action. This rig file is extremely exposed so that viewing and dissecting this setup is much easier.

10.4 Cover Image

The completed front cover image for this book was created using Autodesk 3ds Max for all of the visual components and then enhanced, compiled and finished in Adobe Photoshop CC (Figure 10.2).

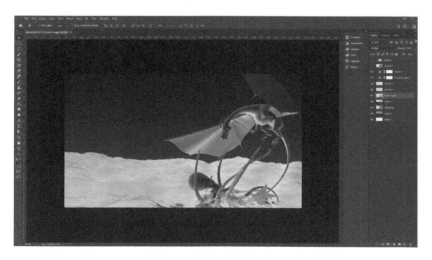

Figure 10.2

Adobe Photoshop CC was used to composite the render images from Autodesk 3ds Max to create the final front cover image.

As it is completely out of the scope (and focus) of this book to discuss how to use Photoshop, it is important to remember that the core images were created and rendered using 3ds Max only. The creatures themselves are simply the final files that we created throughout this text and they were merged into the same scene and posed as you can see in that final image.

The water was created using a simple *Plane* geometry with a number of *Noise*, *Push* and *Relax* modifiers added to it. There's really nothing complicated going on there at all!

Materials for the image were created in 3ds Max and use the standard built-in materials that are available to everyone with just a few changes to the default values. Arnold materials were actually used, as all rendering was done in the built-in Arnold rendering engine… Actually, I switched over to Default Scanline rendering when grabbing the wireframe renders, but that was for speed and easy access, mostly.

Final compositing was done in Photoshop, as I've already said. This allowed me to edit the hue and saturation of the final image as well as changing the colors, as the default output of gray was less than appealing.

10.5 Digital Creature Rigging

The *Digital Creature Rigging* series is something that I've been wanting to work on for a long time. The first book, *Digital Creature Rigging: The Art and Science of CG Creature Setup in 3D*, was something I'd originally wanted to do in 2007. But, life got in the way and productions took up most of my time. It wasn't until 2011 that I started writing it, and it was published internationally in 2012. It was a big achievement for me, and the extra time it took me to get around to actually writing it allowed for me to improve my techniques and various methods so that I was able to deliver a publication that I thought (and still think) was pretty great. In fact, the book was even translated into other languages, so it's really great to think that those who read and speak other languages get to be part of this *Digital Creature Rigging* series, too.

Both of the books I have written rely only on Autodesk 3ds Max and nothing else. This means no plugins, no scripts, no extras that need to be found or purchased and no chance that something might not work anymore. Obviously I can't futureproof for changes to the core foundations and architecture of 3ds Max, but I'm happy to say that the techniques in 2012 are still completely valid right now – October 2018 at the time of writing this.

At the time that the first book was published, 3ds Max was software that was often forgotten about when it comes to rigging, and sadly I think that's still the same now, as Maya is more widely adopted in my experience. Now, that's not to say that amazing rigging work is not being done in 3ds Max; it has, it is and it will continue to be created on every part of this planet. But in terms of available resources, things are limited in the 3ds Max space in comparison to others out there. However, I hope that this book helps to bridge some of the gaps, and there are of course other resources both in print and online that are also amazing to reference and follow. Thank you to all the contributors who share their knowledge and skills with the rest of the world and those still learning, just like me.

10.5.1 The Creature Collection

Digital creature rigging is all about creatures and the rigs that power and drive them. I know, the name is a give-away, but there's nothing quite like being completely obvious! Joking aside, this series has provided us with three unique creatures, each with their own strengths, weaknesses, challenges and visual appeal. These creatures are Belraus, Pheridan and Xilteor (Figure 10.3).

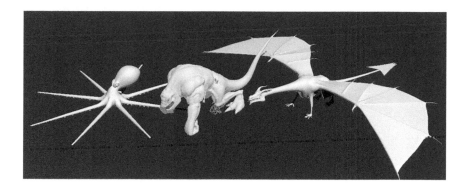

Figure 10.3

Belraus, Pheridan and Xilteor, the three creatures featured in the *Digital Creature Rigging* series of books.

These creatures may have been built and completed many years apart, but they belong in the same universe and share similar principles throughout. What's great about all of these is the fact that they were all built to show specific rigging tasks and challenges for us to overcome, giving us a diverse overview of rigging procedures in the 3ds Max program. All three of them, including their stages of development, are available for free from the companion website (www.DigitalRigging.com), so even without having access to this book, you can get hold of them, animate them, analyze them and even dissect the rigging behind the rigs. I hope that this is inspiring and exciting for those new and old to this industry, and that my way of rigging things has helped your way of rigging.

Let's take one final look at these three great characters.

10.5.1.1 Belraus

Representative of a dinosaurlike creature, Belraus was the main (and only) creature feature from the first book in the series (Figure 10.4). The final rig is a completed setup which performs solidly in most situations.

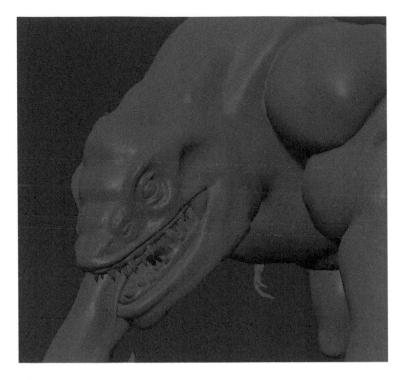

Figure 10.4

Belraus, the creature featured from the first book in the *Digital Creature Rigging* series.

Some of the highlights and features of this creature rig include:

- Overlapping *IK* technique.
- Stretchable limbs.
- Auto-clavicle.
- Snakelike broken jaw setup.
- Custom *Spline IK* spine system.
- Animatable pivot system.
- Muscle system.

10.5.1.2 Pheridan

The giant squid was the first creature that we rigged during this second book (Figure 10.5). A vast change from the dinosaur creature of the first book, Pheridan comes with its own unique challenges.

10. Conclusion

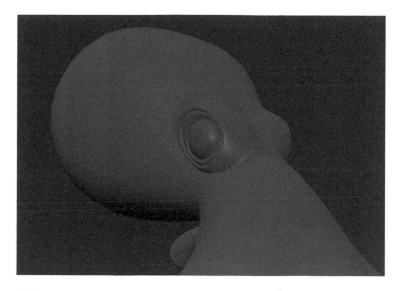

Figure 10.5

Pheridan, one of two creatures featured from the second book in the series.

Some of the highlights and features of this creature rig include:

- Custom *FK* system.
- Multiple limb setup options.
- Automated swimming controls.

10.5.1.3 Xilteor

The huge dragon is the final creature that we rigged in the second book (Figure 10.6). Although sharing similarities with Belraus, we used different techniques for the spine as well as spending time creating automated setups for the wings.

Some of the highlights and features of this creature rig include:

- Custom geometry spine rig.
- Automated wing flapping.
- Automated wing folding.
- Automatic overlapping action in the wings.

10.5.2 The Missing Book

Not exactly missing, but the book *Mechanical Creations in 3D: A Practical Look into Complex and Technical Setups for Animation & VFX*, covers many topics that are mostly not covered when rigging soft-surface creatures. Things like cogs,

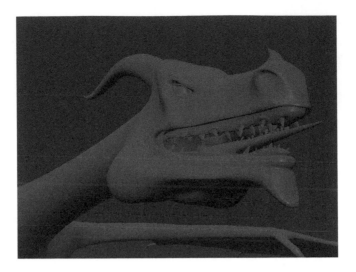

Figure 10.6

Xilteor, the second and final creature featured from the second book in the series of publications.

cranks, wheels, plates, chains, springs and pistons take center stage while rigging a steampunk locomotive. Concentrating on complex and technically challenging structures, this book explains how to apply practical knowledge and methods to combat tricky hard-surface rigging and animation challenges.

This book does not fit into the *Digital Creature Rigging* series, but it does use the same core foundations that this series does. So, if you're interested in increasing your knowledge of hard-surface rigging, this could be a great choice for you. Oh, and you get to rig a crazily complex steampunk locomotive named Norah.

10.5.2.1 Norah

The main focus of the book is the Norah steampunk train that includes many complex and technical areas where we go into setups that are often not needed for soft-surface rigs like those of the creatures in this book. In fact, the Norah locomotive is surprisingly complicated, using a single controller which powers the engine of the train including automating pretty much everything else that needs to be rigged (Figure 10.7).

Some of the highlights and features of this mechanical rig include:

- Automated engine pistons.
- Automated wheel rotations.
- Stretching wires, chains, pipes and suspension.
- Soft, squishy tires.
- Custom setups for various hard-surface rigging challenges.
- Mathematically based problem solving and built-in solutions.

Figure 10.7

The mechanical steampunk train from the "missing book" is a complex locomotive named Norah.

10.6 Closing Remarks

As my role in the creative sectors (film, TV, games, immersive, etc.) have evolved over the years, it has been fascinating to jump back into the rigging process once again. Coming up with various options and solutions to common creature setup problems has been a lot of fun. But, this book has come to its close, and as such we'll be leaving Pheridan and Xilteor behind in these pages. If you've been here from the beginning of the series, thank you for reading the first book and a super thank you for reading this, the second one. If you joined us late and only started with this book, my thanks to you as well, but you should grab hold of that first book, too! I really hope that this was a fun, interesting and informative read for you, and I'd be delighted if I have given you some new tricks and inspiration for working on your own rigs.

I must once again thank my partner in rigging crime, Chris, for creating yet more creatures for us to work with throughout this book. Thank you, buddy. Be sure to check out both Chris's and my links in the Contributor and Author pages at the beginning of this book.

So, my journey with creature rigging has drawn to a close, but hopefully yours is just beginning. Should you or your productions need any consultation, please feel free to get in contact with me and we can hopefully work together in the future.

Farewell, goodbye and good luck! I'll see you around. ☺

Index